DOWNSHIFTING

DOWNSHIFTING

HOW TO WORK LESS AND ENJOY LIFE MORE

JOHN D. DRAKE, PH.D.

BERRETT-KOEHLER PUBLISHERS, INC.
San Francisco

Berrett-Koehler Publishers, Inc.
450 Sansome Street, Suite 1200
San Francisco, CA 94111-3320
Tel: 415-288-0260   Fax: 415-362-2512
Website: www.bkconnection.com

Ordering Information

Individual sales. Berrett-Koehler publications are available through most bookstores. They can also be ordered direct from Berrett-Koehler Publishers by calling, toll-free; 800-929-2929; fax 802-864-7626.

Quantity sales. Special discounts are available on quantity purchases by corporations, associations, and others. For details, contact the "Special Sales Department" at the Berrett-Koehler address above.

Orders for college textbook/course adoption use. Please contact Berrett-Koehler Publishers toll-free; 800-929-2929; fax 802-864-7626.

Orders by U.S. trade bookstores and wholesalers. Please contact Publishers Group West, 1700 Fourth Street, Berkeley, CA 94710; 510-528-1444; 1-800-788-3123; fax 510-528-9555.

Printed in the United States of America

 Printed on acid-free and recycled paper that is composed of 85 percent recycled waste, including 10 percent postconsumer waste.

Library of Congress Cataloging-in-Publication Data
Drake, John D., 1928–
  Downshifting : how to work less and enjoy life more / by John D. Drake.
      p. cm.
  ISBN 1-57675-116-3
  1. Work—Psychological aspects.   2. Quality of life.   I. Title.
  BF481 .D69 2000
  158.7—dc21   00-011786

First Edition

03   02   01   00   10   9   8   7   6   5   4   3   2   1

Designed by Detta Penna

for my brother Bob

*a devoted family man, athlete,
and expert commonsense bridge player,
who is gifted with a warm and generous nature*

CONTENTS

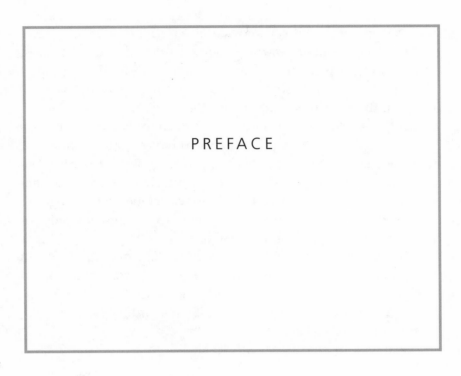

PREFACE

This book is for you if you are

- fed up with the 12-hour work day and want to cut back.
- scared about the risks that come with working less.
- looking for more satisfaction in life.
- making a good income, but wondering if the price is worth it.
- questioning "Is this all there is?"
- wanting more time for your family or yourself, but uncertain about the best ways to achieve it.

Downshifting is all about getting off the merry-go-round. It is written to help you move from the fast track to a more satisfying, less work-focused lifestyle.

You will not find *Downshifting* to be pie-in-the-sky. Most of us need to work to earn a living. We recognize, too, that work can be a positive experience—it can provide us with a sense of self-worth, pride of achievement, and even an identity. But, as with most things in life, dependence on just one source for fulfilling our psychological needs narrows the opportunities for personal satisfaction. This book helps you to expand the possibilities.

In *Downshifting* you will learn ways to cut back and still make a good living. I will show you how to convince your organization that the changes you want to make will be good for the organization. You will even learn how to cope with the scared feelings that you're likely to experience. This book will guide you through all you need to know, and do, to find more free time—not only for yourself, but those you care most about.

I've written this book because I want to share my experiences in becoming a happier, more balanced person. As a workaholic I knew it would be difficult to work less and as a psychologist I knew why, but I learned how to do it—peacefully and profitably. I've never had the desire to go back.

Chapter 1 begins our adventure. Shall we start?

John D. Drake, Ph.D.
Kennebunkport, Maine

Downshift *vi.* (1) To change voluntarily
to a less demanding work schedule
in order to enjoy life more

(2) To shift a vehicle into a lower gear

ACKNOWLEDGMENTS

I would like to express my appreciation to all those who were so willing to give their time to contribute to this book. My gratitude to:

- The Drake clan—JoAnn, John, Kathy, Peter, Rob, and Tim—for their critiques and suggestions. Also dear friends—James Cabrera, Viviana Gentile, Holly Howden, Herman and Dorothy Krone, Val Marier, and Charles Peers.

- My neighbor, Virginia Ray, whose editorial expertise clarified and sharpened the content.

- The willing subjects who shared their lived-out downshifting experiences—Susan Arledge, Andy Basset, Tom and Lynn Bete, Amy Christianson, Peter Drake, Rob Drake, Bob Duncan, Larry and Maureen Filicult, Barbara Goldstein, Tom Himple, Marie Hoffmann, Dave Ketcher, Vince Miello, Margie Pendergrass, George Ostler, Regina Trombitas, Trish Williams, Janet Wittenauer, and Sebastian Yates. Thanks also to the many who provided their stories but desired to remain anonymous.

- My agent, Bill Christopher, who found the ideal publisher for this book.

- My publisher, president of Berrett-Koehler, Steve Piersanti, who took the time to describe to an uncertain author exactly how the book's focus needed to be sharpened.

- My reviewers, whose thoughtful suggestions improved the quality of the text—Frank Basler, Cliff Hakim, Maryanne Koschier, Gates McKibbin, and Jennifer Meyers.

- And last, but certainly not least, my wife Dee Drake—on her fifth book. Once again she read every word and provided countless constructive suggestions.

If I have inadvertently forgotten anyone, please forgive me.

My heartfelt thanks to you all.

IS THIS ANY WAY TO LIVE?

There's more to life than work.
OLD ADAGE

WORKING LIKE CRAZY

"I should have left an hour ago." "Between my job and my family, I haven't got a minute for myself." "The money is great, but there's got to be more to life than this." Do these statements have a familiar ring? Maybe you've uttered the same words yourself. If so, you're not alone. *U.S. News and World Report*[1] found that 49 percent of Americans say our society puts too much emphasis on work and not enough on leisure. For many, the idea of leisure is a joke. Gates McKibbin, a former organization effectiveness consultant with McKinsey & Company, put it this way:

> The prevailing work ethic in the United States right now demands that people succumb to absurdly escalated expectations of the time and energy that one must invest in work-related activities. The fast pace and pressure to be plugged-in at all times, made

possible by the omnipresent cell phones, voicemail, e-mail, lap-tops, and faxes, fuel the expectation that employees should quite literally be available to deal with work issues 24 hours a day—wherever they are, whatever they are doing.[2]

The lead article in a recent *Barron's*[3] magazine stated that "Glutted with goods, Americans increasingly want 'feel-goods'—cruises, makeovers, golf lessons, and the biggest luxury of all, free time."

The good news is that, in the effort to attain more free time, you're a step ahead of most people. Selecting this book suggests that you've probably been thinking for some time about cutting back at work. You have already crossed an important psychological barrier!

In reading *Downshifting*, you are also making a great start to-ward living a more fulfilling life—a goal sought by many, but all too seldom achieved. This book is designed to guide you through the steps necessary for converting your fondest lifestyle dreams into reality.

WORKPLACE ENJOYMENT ROBBERS

Today a variety of forces converge on us at work, resulting in in-creased pressure and incredible demands on our time. Some of these forces are subtle, others overpowering. It is difficult to escape them. I think of these pressures as enjoyment robbers and we are going to explore some of them in this chapter. Quite likely, their presence in your organization accounts for your desire to down-shift.

The Competitive Pressures

One reason we are enjoying our jobs less arises from the impact of the global economy. Competitive pressures bring more mergers and downsizing, and with them a double whammy: the fear of job loss on the one hand and increased work burdens on the other. Margie's story is a case in point:

> Margie is a single mom with two children, ages 7 and 10. She works for a medium-sized insurance company that was recently acquired by an insurance giant. Within one month of the acquisition, two departments were relocated some 800 miles away at the giant's headquarters. While her department of thirty-five was kept in its original location, it was reorganized, and in the process eight jobs were eliminated.
>
> Of course, the term *reorganization* was a euphemism. In reality, the staff was reduced by eight and the work redistributed among the remaining employees. Margie's workload now increased significantly, making it impossible for her to leave each evening in time to cook dinner.
>
> Margie feels afraid that if she doesn't keep up with the new workload she might be terminated. She feels frustrated, too, when working late leaves the children to fend for themselves. She needs the income and is good at what she does, but there's no indication that things will improve. She wonders if she should start "looking."

In a nutshell, competitive pressure forces management to get more productivity from fewer people. While such efforts enhance profits, they also make for long, strenuous workdays that can drive conscientious workers into the ground. "I work half-days—12 hours!" is a jest heard in many offices.

How bad is it for you? Check out "Signs of Overwork" for a list of symptoms characteristic of overworked individuals. Put a checkmark before any of those that describe you. If you checked five or more of these items, you're probably overworked—more than likely, your life is out of balance. It can be dangerous for your health and your close relationships, good reasons to examine downshifting possibilities.

SIGNS OF OVERWORK

_____ My family complains about my absence at many evening meals.

_____ I bring work home almost every weekend.

_____ I have uncomfortable feelings about my strong work focus.

_____ At work, I experience frustration about never seeming to get caught up.

_____ I often feel best when I'm busy, whether it's at work or home.

_____ I call into work at least twice while away on vacation.

_____ I postponed or changed my vacation dates at least once during the past year.

_____ I've been quietly harboring a desire to work less and get off the treadmill.

_____ I feel angry about all that my employer expects of me.

_____ Those close to me often express displeasure about my being away so much on business trips.

_____ I feel guilty when I leave work on time.

The Corporate Culture

The subtle influences that impact negatively on how we work are often unspoken. These stem from the corporate culture reflected in the example set by those above us. If, for instance, our boss comes in each Saturday morning, or works until seven every evening, these work patterns soon become the unspoken norm. No one in authority says that you must stay late or be present on Saturday morning, but you feel the pressure to do so. In some organizations, leaving early on the eve of a holiday is frowned upon. Whatever the unspoken pressures are in your organization, they will almost always reduce your freedom and increase the burden of your job.

Pressure to Make the Numbers

In many companies work becomes less tolerable because there is constant pressure to "make the numbers." In these organizations, the implied threat is to make them *or else*. So everyone works hard to look good *now*. Never mind what negative implications current actions may have for the future. If you don't look good now, you may have no future. As one plant manager said to me, "It's phony and degrading—a helluva way to have to work."

As consultant to a major food corporation, I can vividly recall stories about salespeople persuading friendly customers: "Order a carload now. You can cancel the order next week." In this way, many sales managers met their regional quotas. But it was a house of cards, and there came a day some years later when it came tumbling down. The company's stock value plummeted and another firm acquired them.

Pressure to Serve More Customers

e-Mail now makes it possible for workers to be in touch with far more people than ever before. In addition, with this instantaneous new tool each of your customers or contacts expects a more rapid response than in the days of typewriters and copy machines. Communicating with more people, each of whom expects an instant response, often leads to to-do lists that couldn't be completed in an 80-hour workweek.

Rapid Change

We have all heard about the exponential speed with which life around us is changing. This often translates into increased workplace pressure. Because change occurs so rapidly, we feel the need to be on top of things. This manifests itself in the need to be almost constantly in touch. Even when we choose not to check in, others take advantage of our accessibility and call us! You know the pressure to keep in touch has to be strong when golfers carry phones in their golf bags or when work-related calls are made or received during a family night out. As getting away from the job becomes more difficult, our freedom ebbs away.

Symptomatic of today's go-go business world is the growing

effort of advertisers to convince consumers that their products will help bring simplicity back to their lives. The Associated Press[4] put it this way: "Use of the word *simple* in advertising may not be new, but marketers say it is becoming more prominent as Americans try to restore some calm to frenetic lifestyles."

Overwhelming Work Burdens

Many individuals, especially those who work in corporate staff assignments or in the helping professions, find themselves in job situations in which an overwhelming number of tasks confront them. In most cases, they have no control over the workflow; it just keeps coming. Trying harder to keep up seems to attract more work, negating any progress they've made. Often, when extra effort is extended, no appreciation is expressed. If you are in a job such as this, you're in a classic burnout situation. One seminar participant put it this way: "John, I'm so busy that I don't have time even to *think about*, much less plan for, downshifting."

All of these pressures, added to personal ones, can make life frenetic. We work faster, log more hours, eat at our desks, take work home, call in while on vacation, and still fear for our job. Are you angry about it? So are lots of others. You have a right to be upset. And anger isn't the only consequence of work pressures. Fatigue, loneliness, and diminished intimacy with loved ones are also prices we pay. It doesn't have to be that way.

That you want to make a change to get more enjoyment out of your personal life and work is natural and normal. Why wouldn't anyone want more personal freedom to build closer family relationships, improve on health, reach out to others, and pursue activities they enjoy? Sound appealing? If so, come along and I'll show you how to get off this crazy merry-go-round and live a little!

WHERE WE'VE BEEN / WHERE WE'RE GOING

This chapter discusses the many workplace forces that reduce our personal freedom and are beyond our control. It is unlikely they will go away. For this reason, it makes sense to take greater charge of your life. You can to alter the work demands that rob you of time and energy for family and friends, or for pursuing non-work activities. Given today's work environment, it is altogether reasonable to seek some relief.

In the next two chapters, we're going to explore some forces that could hinder your downshifting. It is important to understand these pressures so that you can identify the most constructive ways for overcoming them. After that, we're on our way to taking some action steps!

Questions for Reflection

1. What bothers me most about my current job and/or work climate?

2. If I imagine myself, at 65 or 70, reflecting on my life, what would have been important and what would not? What do my conclusions tell me about planning my life, starting now?

3. Have I shared my dissatisfactions about my current job situation with those I care about (and who care about me)? If not, why not? If yes, how did they react to my concerns? What does their reaction tell me about proceeding further?

4. If I had more personal time available, what is one way I would spend it?

5. How do I stop myself from setting limits on my work?

CHAPTER 2

THE WORK TRAP

Young executives experience a high as they begin their first job. The title, the secretary, lunches with the "big boys," the sense of power, the heady feeling of associating with the affluent— there is something seductive and quickly addicting about all of this.

BARRIE GREIFF AND PRESTON MUNTER, TRADEOFFS: EXECUTIVE, FAMILY AND ORGANIZATIONAL LIFE[1]

WORK TRAPPING PRESSURES

In the last chapter we saw how workplace pressures often make downshifting attractive and desirable. However, to borrow from the vernacular, cutting back "ain't gonna be easy." If you are like most individuals contemplating reducing your work time, anxiety over potentially reduced income is right in the forefront. It's like cutting back on desserts—it may be the healthy thing to do, but you know that you're going to miss the goodies.

Even if income isn't of great concern, the potential for losing some of the positive aspects of your job also tugs at you. Will you have to give up those activities and social interactions that bring satisfaction and fulfillment?

In this chapter, we'll explore two significant forces that conspire to trap us into working too hard and hence make downshifting difficult. They are:

- Contemporary lifestyles
- Work satisfactions

As we explore these two forces, it will be helpful to identify the ones that most strongly influence you. By cataloguing job traps, you'll be able to determine ways to minimize their impact. For my part, I'll assist by describing practical, action steps that will relieve the pressure. Let's start by examining how the world around us traps us in our work.

Buying into The Plan

Believe it or not, the world around you has a Plan for how you should live your life. The media as well as the words and actions of our contemporaries promulgate The Plan. Most of it has to do with priorities and values. We are often unaware how much our thinking and actions are influenced by outside pressures.

During a recent seminar in Kansas City, Vince, a communications firm VP, spoke with me about his desire to live out a long-cherished dream to own a small marina in the Ozarks. He was complaining that he couldn't move ahead on it. I asked him why not.

> *Vince:* John, I still have to put two kids through college.
>
> *John:* Who says?
>
> *Vince:* Well, one's going to be a senior this fall, and the other is two years behind. . .
>
> *John:* Who says? Who says you *have* to put your children through college? Did your parents foot all your college expenses?
>
> *Vince:* Oh, I see what you mean. As a matter of fact, they didn't have the resources to help me at all.

In Vince's social milieu, almost all families provide for their children's college education. It is done without much questioning. This is how his world tells Vince to behave. Most likely, Vince never considered other options like local colleges, partial support, the availability of part-time work, and so on.

I was not, of course, attempting to dissuade him from providing for his children's education. I was simply suggesting that he examine the source of the obstacle that was holding him back from pursuing the marina purchase and to consider alternatives.

Commonplace Constraints

If you are now hesitating to downshift, part of that reluctance may originate in the world's Plan for living—a plan that may or may not be right for you. The key here is being aware of how such influences are constraining you and your decisions. Here are a few such influences:

- *More is better.* The implication is that acquiring things will bring us happiness. Therefore, it's accepted as the norm, even admirable, to seek higher and higher income, bigger houses, more job advancement, and more possessions—the more luxurious, the better. Things are valued over relationships. It is obvious, of course, that the pursuit of "more" requires plenty of money, which in turn drives us to work harder. We justify having little or no time or energy left for other important parts of life like health, family, and relationships on the basis that we need to maintain our income.

- *Buy now, pay later.* "You deserve it." Immediate gratification is a common theme in advertisements. Credit cards make it easy. The idea of saving up for something is seen as old-fashioned. The parallels carry over to relationships. For example, if the marriage has problems, get a divorce. Many hesitate to downshift because they fear loss of ability to have it all now.

- *The customer is always right.* Total dedication is valued. The expectation is that you won't disappoint the customer, that you won't say "No, I can't" and that you don't say "I can't get it right away." The pressure for customer satisfaction is often so strong that downshifting isn't even perceived as a possibility.

- *Look good.* One way in which this value manifests itself is the booming arena of cosmetic surgery that includes facelifts, breast enhancements, and tummy tucks. On the social scene, looking good is often tied to issues of status and prestige, such as belonging to the best clubs, owning a luxury car, living in a certain

section of town, and having an important-sounding job title or
an impressive office. The list is endless. The central culprit is ego.
If it is important for you to look good, then cutting back may be
more difficult. Many fear that others may perceive us as unable
to hack it, or even reject us because we don't share their values
and choose instead to march to a different drummer.

We've mentioned here only a few values that contemporary society promulgates. There are many more that can trap us into
maintaining the status quo (with our job). I hope the four influences just mentioned will stimulate your thinking about other external pressures that are potentially undermining your desire to
downshift. Discussing this issue with close friends and loved ones
may also help bring these forces into perspective.

The preceding thoughts about worldly values should not be
construed to mean that making more money, or having luxurious
things, or getting what you want now, are inherently wrong. It's
just that for many people they do not turn out to be sources of happiness. In Chapter 9 we'll review the ways that individuals achieve
personal happiness and satisfaction.

Let's see now how we can cope with worldly influences.

COUNTERACTING WORLDLY INFLUENCES

If you suspect that contemporary society's plan for living plays a
role in trapping you into continuing to work as you are, there are
ways to counteract that pressure. A constructive first step is to identify clearly the significant influences or values that could impact
your downshifting decisions.

Checking Your Own Values

Look at my "Checklist of Contemporary Values." Carefully consider each value and ask yourself "In what ways has this value impacted my actions and decisions—especially with regard to family,
career, and personal life?" Check all the values that apply. This can
be an interesting and meaningful exercise.

CHECKLIST OF CONTEMPORARY VALUES

Value	Has affected me		
	Not at all	Some-what	A lot
More is better—especially possessions, income, and status. "The one with the most toys wins."	☐	☐	☐
Enjoy it all *now*. Don't postpone gratification.	☐	☐	☐
Looking good is important.	☐	☐	☐
Success is rising up the ladder.	☐	☐	☐
Getting is more important than giving.	☐	☐	☐
Suffering is stupid. Avoid pain if you can.	☐	☐	☐
The customer comes first.	☐	☐	☐
Focus on pleasing self. "It's got to be right if it feels good."	☐	☐	☐
Career satisfaction is more important than relationships. "I can't get involved in a marriage now or start a family; I want to establish my career first."	☐	☐	☐
Getting ahead is more important than staying in a job you enjoy.	☐	☐	☐
A man is the breadwinner in a family.	☐	☐	☐

Other values that impact on you: _____

_____

_____

_____

If you've identified any contemporary values that are shaping your decision about downshifting, it can be productive to check out their validity. Here are two questions to contemplate:

- Does this value lead to decisions and behaviors that are good for me and those I love?

- How much happiness do I see among those who live out these values?

I myself don't observe much happiness in the world out there. Instead, I see failed marriages, broken homes, substance abuse, latchkey children, hostile teenagers, psychological depression, and more. For me, this picture hardly generates confidence in contemporary values as a basis for making lifestyle decisions.

Sometimes awareness of the nature and impact of these forces on your lifestyle is all that is necessary to get past their entrapping quality and get on to downshifting. Taking cognizance of your uniqueness also can help.

Looking at Your Uniqueness

There is no other person exactly like you. There is no other family exactly like yours. What is good for others is not necessarily best for you. Only you and your family can determine that. The best decision for you, and for those you love, may run counter to the world's plan or prevailing behaviors and values.

If you determine that contemporary world attitudes and values are challenging you to continue your present workload, a conscious reevaluation will be productive. What is truly important in your life? Will the pursuit of contemporary values get you there? After such a reevaluation, you may emerge with a more confident feeling about downshifting. Taking the first steps might even become a joyous experience!

COUNTERACTING THE LURE OF JOB SATISFACTIONS

Another force that can trap you into postponing downshifting is the enjoyment you receive from your job. At times, work is hard to beat. It can help you feel good about yourself and be the source of much satisfaction. When work is like that for us, its pull can be strong. Among other things, your job can:

- *Provide a sense of self-worth and importance.* Your job achievements can result in your feeling good about yourself.

- *Be a source of friends and social interaction.* There may be people at work whose company you enjoy. Jo Ann, employed 20 years as a laboratory manager for a major suburban hospital, put it this way:

  > My work group is like another family. Over the years, as one or another leaves, they almost always say "The hardest part (of moving) is leaving my hospital friends behind." You know, four years ago, Andre retired to Florida and once or twice a month we'll buy a card, all will sign it, and we send him our good wishes. We get letters from Andre, too.
  >
  > As I said, we like being with one another. It would be very hard for me to leave them.

- *Become a means of tapping into our talents and aptitudes.* If you're good at selling, for example, it's rewarding to convince an otherwise reluctant customer to buy your product.

- *Provide a sense of identity.* It is a way of establishing your importance. It says something about who you are and where you fit into this world. Persons who are retired often feel uncomfortable when someone asks "What do you do?" The response "I'm retired" doesn't quite cut it.

- *Be a source of recognition.* A salary increase, praise for a job well done, assignment to an important task force, an important job title, and promotions are all tangible signs of acceptance and praise. They make us feel good—feel important and recognized.

- *Provide a sense of security.* Your salary, fringe benefits, and perks establish an economic base. They provide the wherewithal for your lifestyle.

- *Provide a respite from home.* When the home is not providing a peaceful and nurturing environment, the workplace can become a liberating opportunity for distraction from the pain or problems.

More than likely, you are now experiencing many of the above satisfactions that make it difficult to cut back. You may truly enjoy your work, even if it *is* taxing. If a satisfying workplace is making it difficult to downshift, here are some thoughts to help you add other satisfying activities to your life.

You Haven't Lost It All

It does not necessarily follow that by downshifting you will lose the job satisfactions you now enjoy. Some may remain the same, others diminish. But, there is a possibility that some might even be enhanced. For example, by reducing work responsibility you may feel less overwhelmed and more relaxed. You might be more fun to be around, and therefore experience an increased level of acceptance and praise—perhaps not at work, but from loved ones. But, whether at home or work, others are likely to respond favorably to your increased availability.

Here's how Janet Wittenauer experienced it. Janet is married and has two step-children in their twenties. She was director of executive development for a major medical-products firm. She described her downshifting this way:

> Following a major reorganization, I was named director of executive development on the organization development team. Initially, I loved my job. I was good at designing and implementing new processes and successful in helping our organization to develop leadership talent. But, after a major acquisition, more reorganization and cost cutting, the work wasn't as satisfying. My boss and I had conflicting views and I became disillusioned with senior management.
>
> As I approached 40, a reevaluation began. I gradually became aware that I really wanted to serve others as a coach and consultant, independent from any one corporation. After some internal soul searching, I resigned and went into business for myself—I started my own consulting firm. Of course, I experienced a big drop in income (it is still less than before), but the gain was that I got my life back. I rediscovered my family, and even became a great cook! My husband is happy to have my attention and our friendships and family relationships have deepened. Aside from coaching and consulting, I have become more actively involved in my church and with a couple of community organizations. Right now, life is more whole and enriched than it has ever been.[2]

Focus on the Potential Gain

Most lifestyle changes involve tradeoffs. We trade some career satisfactions in order to bring new dimensions to our life. A good example is Janet's comment about life being "more whole and enriched than it has ever been." A key question then may be: What is it you're seeking? People I know who have downshifted found that while some sacrifices were necessary, the payoff was more than worth it. It could be that way for you as well.

WHERE WE'VE BEEN / WHERE WE'RE GOING

We have been looking at how contemporary values and current job satisfactions can make downshifting more difficult. I mentioned how the world's plan encourages us to have it all now and how work satisfactions provide us with a sense of self-worth and the means to use our talents.

We pointed out the importance of identifying which worldly values and job satisfactions, if any, are influencing you, so that you can more readily find ways to minimize their impact. We suggested you question the validity of these pressures in light of your own uniqueness.

In the next chapter, we will look at how your fears can become a barrier to downshifting. And, as with this chapter, we'll show you how to surmount these deterrents. After that, we'll be on to action steps you can take to downshift and move down the path to greater life satisfaction.

Questions for Self Reflection

1. Which of the contemporary world values has been the strongest in shaping my life or lifestyle thus far? Has it led me to decisions or actions that I now regret?

2. Is the potential loss of some job satisfactions holding me back from proceeding with downshifting? Is it possible that I won't lose any job satisfactions when I downshift?

3. What is important in my life right now? To what extent will downshifting allow me to pursue it?

CHAPTER 3

WHAT'S STOPPING YOU?

They conquer who believe they can. One has not learned the lesson of life who does not each day surmount a fear.

RALPH WALDO EMERSON[1]

COMMON FEARS ABOUT DOWNSHIFTING

Quite often, we are ourselves the real roadblocks to working less. We postpone downshifting, not only because of external pressures (presented in the last chapter) but also by our own internally generated worries. We're fearful because we're contemplating a change; we're trading something we know for something that is less certain. We also realize that risks are involved, and risks are scary. It would be unnatural not to have at least a few concerns about downshifting.

Psychologists tell us that the best way to cope with fears is to confront them. This chapter is designed to help you do just that and to provide ways to surmount them. What follows is a description of concerns that are likely to emerge as you contemplate downshifting. As you read, try to identify those that trouble you the most. Along with each fear, I have provided for your consideration an *On the other hand*. It presents thoughts that may ameliorate some of your concerns. Later in the chapter, I'll discuss additional options to help reduce anxiety about cutting back.

Insufficient Income

One of the major reasons for downshifting is to trade income for time. But that doesn't lessen the worry about money. The questions raised are almost always: "Will I have enough money?" "Will we be able to get by on less?"

On the other hand . . . you may not need as much. Downshifting may result in lower taxes, lower commuting expenses, less need for new clothes, and a different lifestyle. It's possible that any drop in income will be minimal. One of my clients, Seb (Sebastion) Yates, had just such an experience. He told me that he persuaded his boss to allow him to work a four-day week (eight hours less than normal). He said:

> John, the big surprise is that I don't bring home a lot less money than when I was working full-time. My withholding tax, social security, and 401(k) contributions are all lower. You know, I should have done this years ago.[2]

Regina describes how she and her family managed:

> Almost all my life I've been an audio engineer. It's the kind of job that has no time boundaries—you're in that sound studio as long as it takes to get the work completed; around the clock, if necessary.
>
> I'm married and have a 6-year-old daughter, Alyssa. As I watched her grow, it seemed as though she changed before my eyes. When I considered how consuming my job was—how little time I had to spend with her—I felt sad and uneasy. I knew that these formative years were important and precious, and I was missing out on them.
>
> As I was experiencing these uncomfortable feelings, I also began reevaluating my career. I had been an audio engineer since I was 22. The work is challenging and exciting. I was good at it and well

paid. But, where was I going? Would I be doing the same work for another 25 years?

I spoke with my management about future career opportunities within the firm. Their response shocked me. They were unable to describe any pathway for advancement. It struck me that they never even thought that someone like me would want to move upward. As far as they were concerned, I was an audio engineer and that was that!

About the same time, a major brokerage firm offered me an attractive position with a potential salary much higher than what I was making. It was tempting. But, as I thought about it, I realized that I would be right back into working long hours and weekends. I stayed awake most of that night trying to evaluate my situation. It gradually became clear that the time demands in both jobs would keep me from my family. By morning, I knew exactly what I was going to do. I was going make Alyssa, and my husband Richie, my top priorities. I decided to turn down the brokerage firm offer and also quit my engineering job!

After my decision, I felt both scared and exhilarated. In my heart, I knew I was doing the right thing, but we had just bought a new house. With its higher mortgage payments, real estate taxes, and upkeep, how could we manage?

I was determined to make it work, so I set about cutting expenses such as keeping impulse buying minimal and only purchasing what we really needed. I also decided to take a part-time job; it netted me about one-fourth what I was making before, but it enabled me to get Alyssa off to school each morning and usually be there when she got off the school bus.

As Richie became aware that he was now our prime breadwinner, it was a bit of a jolt. For the first time in our marriage, the responsibility was all on his shoulders. Even so, throughout it all he was very supportive.

Despite the drop in our income, our lifestyle really hasn't noticeably changed. We don't save as much as we used to, we spend less, but nothing really essential has been cut back. Somehow we don't seem to need much.

Whatever small sacrifices we've made are more than compensated for by the new-found family time. Apart from the decision to say yes to Richie's marriage proposal, this was the best decision I've ever made. The quality of our life has dramatically improved.[3]

Consider that your own reduced income may actually prove adequate for your needs. Most likely you decided to downshift in order to pursue a different lifestyle. That lifestyle may include a simpler, less possessions-driven way of living, so that your income needs are lower than before the downshift. It's possible, too, because of your scaled back workload, that you might work part-time at something you've always wanted to do (such as teach an evening class), and this could bring supplemental income.

Benefits Loss

A common fear—especially with downshifting efforts that involve working part-time—is the loss of benefits such as medical insurance. This is a valid concern, since benefits may account for 30-40% of your total compensation. The fear is that you will end up with less pay and, at the same time, lose your benefits. All told, that could represent a significant loss.

On the other hand . . . you could choose to cut back only to the extent that you still qualify for health insurance and retirement benefits. Consider, too, that if you take fewer (or no) benefits, you might be able to negotiate for more salary to make up for the loss.

Vulnerability

The fear is that if you are not as work-involved as before downshifting—perhaps not being present as much in the workplace—you may be viewed as dispensable. Perhaps, you think, your downshifted contribution won't be seen as essential.

On the other hand . . . it is helpful to recognize that no one is indis-

pensable. During reorganizations and downsizing all are vulnerable, regardless of rank, contribution, or power. It might even be argued that someone working on a scaled-back basis, perhaps earning less, would more likely be retained.

Reduced Social Stimulation

Being involved in work projects with peers and others is usually stimulating. The exchange of ideas, the camaraderie of teamwork, and the reveling together over a success are all invigorating experiences. Some fear that by reducing their time in the workplace they will miss out on such interactions.

On the other hand . . . you may end up trading some of these office/shop interactions for interactions of another sort. After downshifting you may have more time to deepen relationships with those you love and care about. You may also have more time for community or church activities that bring new social interactions.

Loss of Spark

Going to work each day can be energizing. Having to be at certain places at certain times, or meeting others, can make you feel needed and important. Work demands often keep us "alive" and going. The fear is that you'll miss the stimulation and, as a result, you'll be less efficient or productive.

On the other hand . . . there is no reason to believe that downshifting will result in your being less stimulated. During an interview with Delia Regan, a speech pathologist, she said:

> I was afraid I was going to miss all the client contacts. My work brought me a great deal of satisfaction from working with a variety of people—young children to senior stroke victims. As it turned out, after cutting back I found so many other opportunities for social interaction and challenge that I never missed the reduced client load. I wish I had appreciated that at the time I was considering downshifting. I wouldn't have hesitated for so long.[4]

Losing Out

The worry about losing out is common in people who have Type A personalities. Are you a Type A? Look at the behavior patterns listed next. If you can say "Yes, I'm like that" to four of five of them, you are probably Type A:

- I walk, talk, and eat rapidly.

- I get impatient with the rate at which most things take place.

- I feel vaguely guilty when I relax or am inactive for any extended period.

- I get highly competitive at the thought of someone bettering me.

- I usually try to get more and more done in less and less time.

The "losing out" concern is that others will get ahead of me. The thinking goes like this: "I've worked hard to get where I am. If I cut back time or effort at work, others may pass me on the promotion ladder, and that's troubling."

Another fear the downshifting Type A person often expresses is that "I'll feel uncomfortable with a cutback in responsibilities. I'll get antsy and soon be just as busy as before. I'll be working less and may not be any happier."

On the other hand . . . there is *no "other hand"; downshifting is not going to change your personality makeup.* After cutting back, you'll still be a busy, driven person. The upside is that you'll be busy with more activities of *your* choosing and scheduling. Life could be more satisfying. You may discover, too, that it is easier to let go when you have new goals to strive for or can anticipate new, enjoyable activities.

It has been the experience of many Type A individuals that the competitive drive and the fear of losing out diminish if competitors are not present. If, by downshifting, you become somewhat removed from ambitious peers, you may find that letting go and relaxing come more easily. I have found that my workaholic nature manifests itself in direct proportion to the challenges I see confronting me. When demands are lessened, my drive to achieve falls off. Sometimes, I can even relax and do nothing. (Well, almost nothing!)

No More Promotions?

The fear is that by asking to downshift, I will be perceived as someone whose first priority is *not* the organization. In turn, this could result in my no longer being considered for promotion opportunities and/or developmental activities that could enhance my advancement potential.

On the other hand . . . the organization's loss is your gain. Your shift to a less work-focused lifestyle is exactly what you are about. While it is likely that you will be seen as having less potential, that is not always the case. If you do a good job at your scaled-back assignment, you may still be asked to assume more responsibility or fill a vacancy that requires someone with your technical background or experience.

Here's just one such example. Carl Ottinger is a thirty-something father of three children and a supervisor for a national construction company. His job typically requires stays of two to three weeks per month at construction sites throughout the United States and Canada.

> I came to realize that, despite the great pay, it was a helluva way to live. Work seemed to provide the only satisfaction I got. I was missing out on what I got married for—the companionship of my wife and kids.
>
> I asked the company HR manager to transfer me to our drafting department (located in our offices near my home). I was upfront about it. I said that I wanted to be home most evenings. I explained that I had considerable training in drafting, and that, in the field, I often made creative blueprint changes that pleased our clients or made the construction more cost effective.
>
> It took almost 6 months for an opening to occur. But, when it came, I jumped at the chance and also took a hit on my paycheck.
>
> I have worked in drafting now for almost two years. During that

time something interesting has happened. My practical field experience brought a new dimension to the department. As design problems from the construction sites are reported, the drafting manager has more and more frequently turned to me for solutions.

I have had two pay increases and now, maybe two or three days a month, I travel to building sites to provide help in solving design-related construction problems. My family and I agree that we can live with this occasional travel, and the best news is that it appears that I am next in line to become manager of the department.

I hope that the "on the other hand" comments have already helped diminish your concerns. The next section provides additional help in coping with their impact.

MANAGING YOUR FEARS

Own Up to Your Fears

The first step in managing your fears is to admit that they exist. Your fears will continue to influence your behavior until you admit to them. Ignoring them, in the hope they will go away, is counterproductive.

Talk About Your Fears

Once you admit that you're worried about the consequences of downshifting, a constructive next step is to talk about them. When you talk out your fears, it sometimes results in their almost magical dissipation. It's like having a sleepless night because you're worried about something. You stew over it, but to no avail. Then, the next morning, as you explain your concerns to a friend, the problem doesn't seem as troublesome.

Here are a few ways to make the talking out helpful:

1. *Share your fears with those most likely to be affected by your downshifting.* In most cases, these will be members of your family, close loved ones, or trusted friends.

2. *Focus your discussion around these two topics:*

- *Is the fear justified?* Much as we did in the "on the other hand" sections, question the assumptions you are making about the worrisome issue. You can also examine alternative ways of assessing the risks involved. You may conclude, at least for some fears, that the downshifting gains make the risks worth taking. For example, suppose you are hesitating to downshift for fear of making yourself more vulnerable to a layoff, should the company reorganize or downsize. But the more you explore this potential problem, the more you realize that the company has already had a substantial reorganization, that it's now on an upswing in sales and earnings, and that the likelihood of another downsizing is minimal.

- *How valid is your fear?* As you discuss your concerns, determine whether it originates from within you or from patterns of the contemporary world. If it's from the world around you, evaluate its meaningfulness for your unique life and family situation. How does it fit into your own personal values? Amy's experience provides a good example of how talking out fears can be healing.

When we hold our fears before us at arms length, we are in a position to examine them more objectively, to test their appropriateness and logic, and to discover solutions!

Amy moved up rapidly in her firm and now, at 46, heads the information systems department. With over ninety staff members to direct, frequent corporate restructuring, and several major upgrades in the company's computer system, her job is a pressure cooker.

During the past ten years, as several promotions provided accolades and increased Amy's salary, she pushed aside her underlying resentment about her job's consuming demands. As she conquered one problem after another, she experienced a sense of excitement and achievement, but also became increasingly aware that she never seemed to have a minute for herself. Finding time for even simple activities like banking or reading was difficult.

Recently, Amy's pastor asked her to take responsibility for directing her church's music ministry. Being both an accomplished pianist and organist, Amy knew she would enjoy the assignment. But, she was afraid to commit to the evening hours required for rehearsals. She believed that she should always be available to cope with the frequent departmental crises and, if she were not, her boss might interpret it as a signal that she wasn't that committed anymore.

As Amy discussed her dilemma with two of her closest friends, they helped her realize that her fears were unfounded because she had several highly skilled managers who were quite capable of solving most problems. For a variety of reasons, Amy gradually came to the conclusion that her boss wouldn't think less of her because she wasn't working late most evenings.

Her most interesting insight, however, was the recognition that she really didn't care if he thought less of her for not always being available. The options for solving her dilemma were right in front of Amy, but she gained the insight only after openly discussing her concerns with her friends.

Amy had given her all to the company, and now she thought "It's the time for me." She remembered thinking "If not now, when?" As she talked out her fears, she was able to put them aside and made the decision to downshift—to accept the music ministry and carve out more time for herself.

3. *Speak with a counselor.* While objectively discussing your fears can be helpful, sometimes they are so deep-rooted and emotional that it takes professional help to free yourself from them. If you want to downshift, and talking with acquaintances isn't helping, consider contacting a clinical psychologist for assistance in working through your concerns.

See That Change Is Not Irrevocable

If a job change doesn't work out, it doesn't mean that you'll never be able to go back to what you were doing before, or even go on to something better! Just because you are downshifting doesn't mean that you'll lose your intellectual abilities, personality, or motivational strengths. You'll still be the same talented individual you were before.

Test the Water First

If you are scared about making a significant change, perhaps you can try it out on a preliminary basis. For example, if you would like to telecommute so that you work at home four days a week, try to work out an arrangement in which you begin telecommuting only one or two days a week. Most of the time, just getting started in a new activity helps us clarify and define more precisely what we want. At other times, first steps often take on a life of their own and guide us to our destination. George is an example:

> George was the president of a small suburban bank, but his passion was antiques. George dreamed of owning an antique shop in Vermont. He talked about it ad nauseam. One day I said to him "Please don't tell me any more about your antique shop, just do something about it. Why don't you open a small shop in your garage?"
>
> The words must have sunk in because several months later George emptied his large garage and talked up his weekend antique business. Almost at once, his friends (including my wife and me) brought him items long stored in our attics. "Is it worth anything?" we asked.
>
> Shortly thereafter, an insurance company asked him to appraise a few antiques that a townsperson wanted to insure. Apparently, insurance folks talk with one another because soon other insurance companies began asking him to conduct appraisals. Well, you can probably guess the rest of the story. George quit the bank, enlarged his garage antique shop, and is now working full-time in a business he loves.
>
> He still hasn't moved to Vermont, but he promises that will happen soon.

Note That Inaction Is Also Risky

If you put off downshifting, there is no guarantee that while you delay your job demands will lessen. In fact, they could get worse. Staying put could also mean placing your health, family relationships, and personal happiness at risk. Not taking any steps toward downshifting may be easy, but inaction postpones the opportunity to find more time to enjoy all that life has to offer. How long do you have?

ONE MAN'S STRUGGLE

I want to share with you now the way I came to grips with the fear of making my own downshift. I hope you will find it helpful. So that you can understand the inner drives I struggled with, the story begins immediately after I finished graduate school.

My first job was perfect for a newly graduated Ph.D. I was the organizational psychologist for Allied Chemical (now Allied Signal) and enjoyed it because the job allowed ample opportunity to apply my professional training.

However, as time went by I became aware that, as a human resources specialist, there was little likelihood of my advancing up the corporate ladder. Chemical engineers with extensive manufacturing or sales experience populated top management, so I knew that in order to advance (my very strong desire) I would eventually have to work elsewhere. After five years I decided to seek a job that would provide a career path for me to become the organization's president.

I left Allied and joined a consulting firm that had its roots in psychology, thus it was an organization in which my professional skills were in the mainstream.

After working five years for this human resources consulting firm, I then managed a similar, but smaller firm for two years. But, I still was not content. The dissatisfaction seemed to arise from my having to be accountable to others. I came to the realization that I really wanted to call my own shots, to be my own boss.

So, at age 35, I cut the corporate umbilical cord and started my own consulting firm. I loved it! I made the decisions, set the pace, and reveled in the autonomy.

For the next eleven years I put all of my focus and energy into building the firm. This involved long workweeks, constant travel, brief vacations and, on most weekends, a briefcase full of work brought home.

At the time I accepted all of this, not always happily, but I believed what I had heard—that this is how you "make it," this is how you become successful. And according to contemporary society, I was very successful.

As the years went by we built a fine professional reputation and added offices throughout the United States. The firm, Drake Beam & Associates (now Drake Beam Morin) became the nation's largest human resources consulting firm.

Here it was. The dream had become a reality. My own company, posh Park Avenue headquarters, good income, large suburban home, new cars, the best education for my children, status, power—all that I had ever hoped for. Indeed, more than I ever imagined was mine.

But something was missing.

One day my wife said to me "Jack, when are you going to take time to smell the roses?" I was about 46 at the time and was quite receptive to her comment. For two years I had been privately pondering similar questions.

As I mentioned, travel seemed to be inescapable. I spent many hours alone on planes. It was my quiet time, a time away from the hubbub of the office, a time to think and reflect. I kept pondering my situation. I seemed to have everything. Why was I not more happy and satisfied? What was missing? Frequently I found myself asking "Is this it? Is this all there is?"

For nearly three years I struggled with these thoughts and uncomfortable feelings. When I related my discontent to others, in contrast to the encouragement that Amy received from her friends, I found little support or understanding. My friends said, in effect, "What you've got is what we're all striving for. How can you complain?"

I now began to question myself. Maybe it's me, I thought. Maybe I'm just a malcontent and nothing will make me happy. I wanted to take some corrective action, but I wasn't sure of what to do.

The answer was slow in arriving. (It seems so obvious to me now, but at the time, I couldn't see it.) The breakthrough insight about what was missing in my life was spawned by the constant travel. I would wake up mornings in a hotel room and ask myself "What am I doing here? I miss my wife, I miss my kids, hell, I'm missing out on life!"

As I reflected on it, what friends did I have? I never really had the time, or even the inclination, to cultivate friends outside the circle of my business associates. I always seemed to be caught up with company concerns; more often than not, they disrupted our family activities and plans.

Sure, I was the boss, and perhaps I created some of the business demands, but whatever the case, the job pressures and my worka-holic nature seemed to keep me from doing what I now realized I wanted to do—build deeper relationships.

About this time (I was now 49) my wife found a letter I had written to her fifteen years earlier. It had been written in a hotel room, and it said (in part):

> "I am lonely and miss you. This is no way to live, and
> when I get back to the office I am going to figure out
> some way to cut back on this traveling. I want to spend
> more time with you and the boys. . ."

The day my wife found that letter, I could have written one ex-actly like it. Fifteen years had passed and nothing had changed. I vowed, then and there, I was going to do something about it.

But what to do? One thought was to appoint myself chairman of the board and play a less active role. But, I knew my predilec-tion for getting involved. Having nurtured the company, I doubted that I could take a back seat. I came to the conclusion that if my life were to change I would have to remove myself from the scene, so I decided to find a buyer for the company.

But then fear manifested itself. Suppose I gave it all up—the title, power, income, status—and it didn't work out? Suppose Dee remains committed to her activities and there isn't much more time for us to be together? Suppose the closeness I sought with her and the children didn't materialize? I felt troubled and scared, truly scared. It immobilized me.

At that time, a fortunate event occurred. We attended a World Wide Marriage Encounter Weekend. That weekend helped me learn that the "more" I was seeking could be achieved, that a more intimate relationship with Dee could be had. The biggest surprise, however, was the discovery that my basic psychological needs could readily be met within our relationship; it wasn't necessary to rely on my business activities to gain the acceptance and recognition I enjoyed. That weekend was a turning point because it helped me to get past my fears. It was not long before I found a buyer for the company.

I'll never forget the day I announced to the staff that I was going to resign as CEO and change my lifestyle.

I told them that I was going to sell the house that had seemed so important to me and move to a smaller house in Maine. I was going to do some things I had been wanting to do for fifteen years: spend more time with our late-in-life gift, our seven-year-old, and write some books that I've had in my head for many years. Oh, I suggested, I would still do some consulting, but not just any projects. I would try to select some of the interesting and challenging assignments I had to pass by because of management responsibilities.

I told them I was going to spend more time being a lover to my wife and a better father for my children. I told them I was going to take time to smell the roses.

I must confess, though, that when I got to the part of my speech where I was to say ". . .and, therefore, effective December 31, I will resign as CEO," the words choked in my mouth; I could hardly voice them. There was much more emotion and latent fear within me than I had realized.

So we sold the big house, had a huge "garage" sale to dispose of all our furnishings, and moved to Maine to begin life anew. I had a modest nest egg from the sale of the company, a three-year non-compete clause (with teeth), and no job—just a desire to be together with my family.

On the day we drove away from our old house, our station wagon containing our only possessions, I experienced a euphoric sense of freedom. I felt the way Jonathan Livingston Seagull must have felt gliding and soaring over the waves!

Life took on a beautiful glow. I discovered things about myself that I never believed were there. The biggest surprise was an interest in and satisfaction from reaching out to others. I had never done much of that, except as required by my job. But, now I found myself volunteering and enjoying it.

Our lovemaking became better. Dee put it this way: "This is how sex should be—not rushed and strained, but relaxed, warm, and tender."

There was also a spiritual awakening. I felt a closeness to God I had not experienced before. I found peace in my ability to turn troubling matters over to Him.

I discovered that less is more. With far fewer possessions, less income, and a simpler life, I was much more peaceful. I found enjoyment in quiet walks on the beach, watching sunsets, and spending more time with our youngest child.

I learned that for happiness in my life, a deep love relationship is essential. Dee and I try to make each other Number One in our lives—not the job, not the kids, not the relatives, but each other. When we do that, our priorities are clear and everything seems to fall into its proper place. When it comes to making important decisions, for example, we ask ourselves "Will this bring us closer or pull us apart?" If we decide that it will get in the way of our closeness, we don't proceed.

This focus on each other may appear selfish, but when you think about it, a loving relationship is the best gift you can give your children and the others in your family.

Our move to Maine brought new careers for Dee and me, and our achievement needs kept us busy with work and community activities. But even now, many years after leaving the Big Time, the satisfaction and contentment I sought and found are still being experienced. I have never had second thoughts about the wisdom of my decision to downshift.

I hope it will be that way for you and all who seek better balance in their lives.

As I look back on my life, I realize that there were clues along the way that pointed to what was good for me and what was not. I didn't pay much attention to them because I was distracted by the trappings our contemporary world tells us are so important—possessions, power, and prestige. There are signposts in your life as well. If you reflect on your life experiences, perhaps you'll find the power to overcome any doubts you may have about downshifting.

READINESS

One final, self-generated downshifting obstacle should be mentioned. That obstacle is psychological readiness. I was in my early fifties when I made the big decision to downshift; I doubt I could have done it in my early thirties because I wasn't ready yet. Maybe my lifestyle wasn't hurting enough or perhaps my business success was too rewarding.

There are stages in our adult life in which downshifting is more appropriate than it is in others. For example, it is one thing to work exorbitant hours when you are twenty-something; it's quite another if you are a parent in your forties. Sometimes, too, if we've just made a significant life change (new job, for instance) we usually need a stabilizing period before moving to a new stage. If you are hesitating to downshift, consider, among the fears already mentioned, your readiness to advance to a new level of adult growth. If you suspect that you are clinging to status quo, you may find Gail Sheehy's book *Passages*[6] to be helpful reading.

WHERE WE'VE BEEN / WHERE WE'RE GOING

This chapter highlighted the importance of confronting your fears or doubts about downshifting. To assist you in this confrontation, I provided a list of common concerns, along with suggestions for surmounting them. Mentioned were the importance of:

- Admitting your fears
- Talking about them
- Recognizing that no job change is irrevocable
- Testing or trying out a change
- Realizing that inaction also has its risks

I hope you are now ready to begin steps toward downshifting. If not, the next chapter will help you with any indecision you still may be experiencing.

Questions for Reflection

1. Who would be the best person(s) with whom to share my worries or fears about downshifting? When would be a good time to meet with them?

2. Deep down, what is my greatest concern? How do I feel about confronting it? How uncomfortable will it be to share it with someone else?

3. What are the risks and gains for downshifting? If the risks are greater than the gains, what am I willing to do? If the gains are greater than the risks, what am I willing to do?

4. What feelings are being experienced as I answer these questions?

CHAPTER 4

MAKING THE DECISION

Not to decide is to decide.

Laurence J. Peters, *Peter's Quotations*[1]

THE TIME PROBLEM

"John, I'd love to downshift, but I haven't got the time even to think about it!" For many, finding time is a formidable obstacle to changing their lifestyle. Working twelve-hour days and six-day weeks doesn't leave much time for making an important decision about cutting back, much less the necessary time for planning.

If you are trying to decide about downshifting but are so stressed out or time-pressured that getting to it seems impossible, this chapter is for you. We'll describe steps that have worked for others in similar circumstances; I hope they will enable you to make the right decision.

If you've already made your decision, you can skip ahead to Chapter 5. There you will find a variety of low-risk downshifting options.

The first significant step to make downshifting a reality is to carve out sufficient time for thinking about it.

CREATING SPACE

Let's accept the fact that the time needed for deciding about downshifting is not going to be handed to you. Rather, you will need to create space to think about this life-changing step. Among the items to be considered are:

- Which of the many downshifting options is best for the near term? Long term?

- What is the impact of each option upon your future work life?

- How will you and those close to you manage potential lifestyle changes—the good and the bad?

- What are the foreseeable obstacles to implementing a plan?

Such an analysis takes time, lots of it. Here are some ideas to get you started.

Take Time Out

If you are caught up in the rat race, grabbing a few quiet moments on the weekend or on the commute home is not likely to be adequate. For important, critical decisions, you owe it to yourself and your loved ones to give them patient, focused consideration. Where will you find this kind of time? You have to make it:

- Schedule early-morning or evening quiet times.

- Take an extra two days after a weekend.

- Carve out vacation time.

- Ask for a sabbatical.

- Take a week of "personal time."

During your "time out" period, consider seeking solitude. Current research suggests that most people have some need for time alone to satisfy any of several psychological needs, including rejuvenation. Those who need it the most are those with heavy demands on their attention, social skills, or coping mechanisms—such as health care providers, middle managers, and mothers of small children. Does your life have these demands? If so, you might consider making a two- or three-day retreat. It's easy to do. You could go to a spa, bed-and-breakfast, resort hotel, camping facility, or nearby retreat house. It doesn't have to be connected with any type of religious organization, although many are held in former monasteries or convents. Jack and Marcia Kelly provide a good source of information about lodgings and retreat houses in their book entitled *Sanctuaries*.[2]

Trish Williams, a married 51-year-old human resources executive, made her downshifting decision in this way:

> As I moved up the corporate ladder, 90 percent of my working day seemed to be occupied with administrative activities. Crowded out were the job activities I most enjoyed—being a practitioner solving organizational problems. I felt unfulfilled, but was uncertain about downshifting. I had worked hard to get to this level of management and was reluctant to give it up.
>
> At this point I took a two-week vacation with my husband in Tahiti. It gave me plenty of time to reflect on my life. I grew more aware of life's shortness and that I was investing my time in ways the corporation wanted, not in the way I wanted. The sense of "something isn't right" came into focus and with it a vision of me taking charge of my life. Then the excitement and momentum began to grow and, one day near the end of my vacation, I made the decision to align my values with how I live.
>
> When I returned to St. Louis, I resigned from the corporation. I have since found freelance consulting in the areas of executive coaching and leadership development to fit my skills, interests, and values.[3]

Not everyone can get to Tahiti, but in addition to the get-aways mentioned earlier, you can locate places for scheduling tranquility in your own home town. Some find it in peaceful walks, or sitting in an empty church, or driving to a quiet park, or even sipping coffee in a busy coffee shop. What works for you?

For a helpful how-to book on creating quality time, consider reading Ruth Fishel's *Precious Solitude*.[4]

Family Meeting

Another way to create space for thinking is to schedule a series of family meetings. In these meetings, involve those close to you who will be affected by your cutting back. In some cases, the meeting might involve only your spouse or partner; in others, the entire family might be present. These discussions are particularly important when your downshifting plans are likely to bring about a significant change (much lower income or a move, for example).

It is easier to assemble the members of your group or family for discussion when they know that the meeting will have a definite time for beginning and ending, and that the duration will be an hour or less. For this reason, it's often better to schedule several half-hour meetings than one long session. The space between meetings can also be productive, as it enables participants to process and reflect upon the topics being discussed. It even gives these people who are important to you time to talk privately among themselves. In this way, deeper, sensitive issues are more likely to be brought up in subsequent meetings.

For the most effective use of everyone's time, each meeting should have a core question that becomes the theme of the discussion. Here are four suggested topics:

- Here's how I am considering downshifting (describe your current thinking) and here's why I'm considering it. What do you think about the idea? What kind of "vibes" or feelings do you have—anxious, happy, fearful, what?

- What are the "what ifs" you're concerned about? For example, "What if I telecommute and set up an office here at home?"

- What do you like the most and the least about the idea of my downshifting? How will life be different for you?

- When would be the best date for me to begin cutting back?

It isn't essential to get agreement on all the discussion questions. The act of talking about the issues is beneficial in and of itself. It can often unify the group and bring family members closer together. In addition, your decision process is aided by the opportunity to view downshifting from different perspectives and to clarify your thinking as you voice your thoughts.

IF YOU'RE STILL "ON THE FENCE"

Suppose you've followed my suggestions: you created some space for yourself, you spent time reflecting on the important issues, and you had your family discussions. But you are still uncertain about what to do. Now what? Here are a few recommendations.

Listen to Your Gut

Perhaps we can't summon to a conscious level all the information stored in our brains, but we need to listen to our intuition because it is rooted in our life experiences. It is worth paying attention to.

Assuming you have intellectually considered the pros and cons of downshifting, how does the act of cutting back *feel*? If it feels good, feels "right," then go ahead. If it feels uncomfortable, feels "wrong," then something at home or at work probably needs to be changed, adjusted, or attended to. Once you determine what that issue is, and then do something about it, take another look at downshifting. This time you may find the decision is easy.

Pray or Meditate

If you normally include prayer in your daily life, talk with God about your dilemma. Ask for the wisdom to help you make the right decision. Then do some listening. Prayers are often answered in quiet moments of silence.

Meditation is another form of prayer. It's a way of listening to what's within. In some quiet space, be aware of all the things that chatter through your mind while you are trying to still it. In the midst of the chatter and the stillness, clarity of direction often follows.

Here's the prayer experience of Tim and Lynn Bete, a thirty-something professional couple who told me that they were such workaholics that "we lived at work":

> We found that when we started to pray we began to change. Prayer slowed us down. More and more we started praying to-gether and that changed our marriage. We slowly realized that our careers, which we thought were so important, were not as impor-tant as family relations. It took us two years to make the decision to change the way we lived. Prayer led the way.[5]

Find the Roots of Your Fear

When we are fearful, it's natural to wonder about the cause of our concern or anxiety. Sometimes the reason is obvious; at other times, though, the source of our fear is obscure. In these cases, we tend to select a reason that seems logical, but, more often than not, it's not the true source of our fear.

One way to test the accuracy of your diagnosis is to ask yourself the question "If I could remove this obstacle, would I be comfort-able in proceeding with downshifting?" If your answer is no, or if you find yourself hesitating, it's likely that you still need to explore other sources of your concern. As I mentioned earlier, talking with trusted friends or family about your worries can help uncover them. Once the source of your fears is identified, it is often possible to plan steps to minimize the problem.

Sometimes it takes an emotional experience—a meaningful psychological event such as a retreat, illness in the family, or spiri-tual conversion—to free you from being trapped by your own logic. An example of such a freeing event was my Marriage Encounter ex-perience (described in Chapter 3).

Focus on the Potential Gains

Sometimes we are indecisive about making a change because fears interfere with our ability to fully appreciate the potential gains. Right now, any number of factors may be impelling you to cut back so you can enjoy life more, but worries about the "what ifs" cloud your vision of the future.

One antidote is to spend some time envisioning all the positive things that could happen after you downshift. Consider the time you might have to

- Pursue favorite interests—painting, sailing, antiquing—activities that you enjoy doing but seldom have time for
- Develop warmer and closer relationships with those you love and enjoy
- Reach out to others and delight in the satisfaction of helping

All of these activities are common among happy people. They can become more a part of your life as well.

It is helpful to list the potential satisfactions to be derived from your downshifting. A chart like "Potential Gains from My Down-shifting" (on the next page) is a convenient format for you to record your thoughts. Keep it handy so you can jot down other advantages that occur to you during the next few days. After a week, review the list privately or with your partner, and take one more pass at making your decision.

Consider the Worst Case Scenario

It is often helpful to ask yourself "What's the worst that can happen?" This usually means reviewing the what-ifs. For example, "What if I leave my job and find that I hate working at home as a consultant?" "What if I end up making half of my current salary?"

By focusing on potential issues, you may conclude that you're not willing to cope with the worst-case possibilities. Or, you may decide that they're not that bad after all and that you'll make out all right, whatever happens.

If none of the above suggestions have helped you to decide, peacefully accept that, while your current work situation is not satisfactory, you won't let it weigh you down. Be comfortable with the fact that it's the best you can have right now. At a later time, you can revisit downshifting. In fact, set a target date for taking another look at changing your lifestyle.

POTENTIAL GAINS FROM MY DOWNSHIFTING

Gain	Near-term	Long-term
1.		
2.		
3.		
4.		
5.		
6.		
7.		
8.		

WHERE WE'VE BEEN / WHERE WE'RE GOING

This chapter was designed to help you move forward in making a decision about downshifting. It pointed out that a major obstacle to cutting back is finding the time even to think about it. In most cases, moving ahead with downshifting will require conscious effort to create some space and some quiet time for reflecting and planning.

Once you've allocated some time to think about downshifting, find the value of scheduled tranquility—a quiet time for leisurely thinking.

Three suggestions were also provided for "getting off the fence": listen to your gut reactions, pray/meditate, and focus on the potential gains. If none of these work, consider setting a target date to examine the feasibility of downshifting once again.

If you've already said "Yes, I'm ready," you'll find the next chapter most interesting because it talks about low-risk ways for downshifting.

Questions for Reflection

1. If I were to create some space for myself, when and how could I do it?

2. To what extent have I asked those close to me to review the pros and cons of my downshifting? How helpful would it be to set up a family meeting?

3. If I put off downshifting now, when would be the best time to revisit the idea?

CHAPTER 5

LOW-RISK DOWNSHIFTING OPTIONS

What if we put in shorter hours and got the work done anyway?
Don't laugh. Some people are doing it.

AMY SALTZMAN[1]

GETTING THE LIFE YOU WANT

It has been said that the time we make available for work is infinite and the time for everything else is finite. True, isn't it? We almost always make time for the job: we change schedules, postpone vacations, work late, or bring the work home. Somehow the job gets done, while the time for self or family is pushed aside or postponed.

If you are reading this chapter, I'll assume you've decided to do something about work's incursion on your personal life. From a broad perspective, you can take three different approaches to provide more time for yourself and family. They are:

- Stay in your present job and adjust the way you manage your workday.

- Stay in your present job and restructure your work arrangements.

- Leave your job and strike out on a new path.

This chapter discusses the first option.

CHANGING THE WAY YOU WORK

For many people, the burden of work is so consuming and fatiguing that little or no energy is left for life off the job. Sometimes, by creating more time for self during the workday, you can reduce fatigue and address personal needs more fully. This chapter provides ten suggestions, many of which are relatively easy to implement. However, as with all job changes, there are inherent risks. I'll suggest some steps to help you keep them to a minimum.

Keep Lunch Time Personal

"Why don't we get together for lunch?" is almost an automatic phrase for some of us. For many, lunchtime is part of the workday. It can range from a planning meeting over sandwiches at your desk to taking a client to a fancy restaurant.

Instead of working during lunch, you could spend the time for personal needs—making personal phone calls, getting your hair done, exercising at a fitness center, visiting a friend, or simply taking time out to rest or relax. If lunchtime activities such as these would result in more time (or energy) for self and family, then freeing up your lunch hour could be a productive step.

IMPLEMENTATION:

It is usually best to make this modification in stages. Start by selecting a particular day of the week, and gradually designate more lunchtimes as *your* time. Make a point of blocking off the time on your calendar and be sure that your secretary or staff know which lunchtimes are "taken."

Set More Reasonable Deadlines

Often we make our own crises. Especially if we have a Type A personality, we think almost everything has to be done *now*. We believe that if we tell our boss that the project can be ready sooner than anticipated, we'll look good. Maybe so. But the stress of an unrealistically early deadline can also result in less than optimal performance on other ongoing work efforts.

This option suggests that you consciously avoid the trap of believing that everything has to be done today or tomorrow. When asked "When can I expect it?" add time to your answer so that you reasonably account for unforeseen contingencies and a peaceful pace. A principle that works for me is to double the time I estimate will be required.

This reasonable deadline approach applies to phone calls as well. Some phone calls, for example, don't need to be returned today, or even tomorrow or next week!

IMPLEMENTATION:

In her book, *Simplify Your Life*,[2] Elaine St. James suggests that we factor into our planning schedule at least an hour each day for "unproductive" time. This accounts for interruptions that get in the way of meeting deadlines: telephone calls, unplanned meetings, searches for misplaced papers, unexpected visits from co-workers, and other time robbers. Her idea represents a good first step toward setting more reasonable deadlines.

Say No to Some Assignments

For many of us, achievement is a prime source of personal satisfaction. When we get something accomplished, we feel good about ourselves. For this reason it is often difficult to refuse an assignment or work project. Often, we may judge that it is risky to refuse any task.

When evaluating the efficacy of saying no, consider the possibility that you might become even more productive. You might find, for example, that with fewer projects your quality is better or deadlines are more promptly met.

Consider, too, that not all projects are equally satisfying. By rejecting those you dislike, you'll gain time and end up enjoying your work more.

Here are two principles:

- Explain *why* you are turning down the assignment. State your reason simply and without appearing defensive. Recognize that your "no" won't always be perceived negatively. At times, it commands respect. For example, when you say "I'm sorry, but I can't take that project on right now, I have other projects for which I have made a prior commitment," your statement implies that you are a person who is upfront, reasonable, and dependable.

- Whenever feasible, mention a date when you *could* take on the work. This shows your desire to contribute and may soften your boss's feelings of rejection or disarm a perception that you lack commitment.

Declare Your Priority for Family

If time for family or relationships is important to you, say so. When you overtly express your conviction, it will result in others thinking twice before requesting your time over and above the normal workday. It explains, without your continually having to justify yourself, why you don't come in on Saturdays, or do leave promptly at closing time, or zealously guard scheduled vacation time. When you openly declare "My family comes first," word gets around and expectations about your availability change.

Marie is a single parent. She has a 15-year-old son Toby, a star basketball and football player. Most of his games (home and away) are played on Friday evenings. The highlight of Marie's week is watching Toby play, but in order to make the games she must leave the office promptly at 4:30.

Having missed many games because of late-day meetings and last-minute requests for data, Marie resolved to do something about it. She told her boss and others, "Toby is my number one priority, and I need to schedule Fridays so that I can leave no later than 4:30."

Word soon got around. Marie began hearing statements such as "We'd like to get together with you on Friday, but we'll schedule the meeting early in the day, OK?"

To be sure, there were some crisis situations in which Marie stayed late, but these were few. Almost everyone respected her priority for family, and some were even encouraged to make similar requests.

In some organizations, making an overt declaration for family will be applauded; in others, it can be the kiss of death. For the latter, while it is not likely to result in termination, it probably will impact negatively on the company's vision of your potential. This is particularly true in up-or-out organizations or work environments in which ten- to twelve-hour days are expected (and maybe even necessary).

IMPLEMENTATION:
One way to proclaim priority for family is to do as Marie did—make a declaration. For most, however, the announcement can naturally grow out of requests for your time or effort, which you turn down with a statement such as "I'd like to help you out, but I've got a family commitment that makes it impossible." A statement similar to this one, mentioned a few times, will make your point.

Avoid Business Travel on Weekends

One of the first downshifting steps I took was to eliminate out-of-town, Monday morning appointments. When I had to travel on Sunday for a Monday meeting, Sunday became a "lost day" as far as family was concerned. My focus was on packing, organizing my work materials, and getting to the airport on time. I may have been physically present to my family, but mentally my focus was elsewhere.

A variation on this option is to make out-of-town arrangements so that you travel homeward on Fridays, not Saturdays. In fact, the worldwide consulting firm of McKinsey & Company had a policy that required all employees to be in the office on Fridays. This assured that people were home for the weekend.

IMPLEMENTATION:
In organizations that deliberately plan meetings to include a Saturday-night stayover (to keep airfare costs minimal), this may

not be a viable option. This option works best in job settings in which *you* schedule meetings and travel plans.

It may not always be possible to avoid early-Monday or late-Friday engagements, but with conscious effort and a willingness to declare family a priority, you can gain an extra day to enjoy your personal life.

Make Firm Personal Appointments

Put all of your family and other personal commitments on your business calendar and give all items equal priority. If staff schedules your time, instruct them to keep the personal time sacred. Thus, if you plan a luncheon with your spouse on Tuesday, that time is blocked off and not available to others. This is a simple but effective procedure. Failure to install such a scheduling system results in personal and family time being available only if work commitments don't interfere.

IMPLEMENTATION:
It is as simple as writing personal and family dates in your appointment book and taking the steps to see that they don't get changed.

Take Family on Business Trips

Often it takes advanced planning, but what a marvelous way to have time for family, especially if the trip can be scheduled to include a free weekend. Consider, too, taking the family, especially children, to your workplace. Let them see the office or shop, meet some co-workers, and get the flavor of your daily commute. Some companies encourage children's visits by offering special career days or a "take your daughter to work" day. Another opportunity occurs on the eves of major holidays such as Thanksgiving or Christmas. Many workplaces close early and the holiday spirit is conducive to family visitors.

IMPLEMENTATION:
In almost all cases, you will need to pay for your family's travel ex-

penses. Try to select a trip in which the location offers interesting activities while you are working. Another consideration is to inform your client or company representative that your family will be accompanying you. My family experienced many fun-filled, memorable trips in which customers took the initiative to host my family during the day I was working.

Set Stop Lines

Have you ever been working late and found yourself muttering "One more hour and then I'll head home," only to find that two hours later you're still working and still unfinished?

Stop lines are a means of applying the brakes to long hours. They involve setting a time beyond which you will not work (except in a true emergency).

Here's what Bob Duncan, an account manager for Northern Telecom, said about this downshifting option:

> I am a driver. I like to finish whatever I start. While I was accomplishing a lot, I also found that I was losing out on family life. Typically, I would get home at eight o'clock or later. After some upsetting discussions with my wife, I realized that I had to do something about it, and do it quickly.
>
> I decided to work until six each evening and then quit—whether the task was completed or not. It was difficult at first, especially when I thought that another half-hour would finish the job. But when I was tempted to stay I said to myself "It's six and you should be out of here." And so I began stopping at my six o'clock time line.
>
> It's interesting. The work was still there when I came in the next morning, and more often than not, I quickly finished it up—faster than I might have done the night before—and everything went fine.
>
> For me, setting a firm time line, and sticking to it, is the only way I have found that gets me home early and keeps my priorities in order.[3]

IMPLEMENTATION:

Sometimes work demands are such that you can only select certain days of the week to implement your time line. Select which days, and what seems to be a reasonable time line, and then experiment. Try to find the pattern that meets your goals both at home and at work. The key to making this option succeed is being *consistently* firm about leaving once the stop line is reached.

Negotiate Extra Vacation Time

If you are entitled to two weeks' vacation, ask for three or four.

IMPLEMENTATION:

This option is most viable when you are offered a new job; it should be part of your negotiations. If you want more vacation time in your present job, be certain to explain how you will space the time-off so that it is not disruptive. You will need to be clear that you don't expect to be paid for the extra time off. However, I know of several people who got an extra week and the company paid them as though they were at work. The outcome of your request will depend a lot on how valued you are and your position in the company. The higher your position in the organization, the more likely your request will be granted.

Move Closer to Work

It seems ridiculous to spend three or four hours each day commuting to and from work, and yet it is commonplace. We allow ourselves to become slaves to train or bus schedules or to the vagaries of freeway traffic. If you commute, ask yourself "Is it worth it?"

One alternative is to move closer to your present work location. However, if such a change requires moving to an area with out-of-sight housing costs, this option may not work for you. The second alternative is to remain in your present housing and seek new employment in a location (usually less metropolitan) that is less than a half-hour from home. Wouldn't it be rewarding to have time, before dinner, to walk with loved ones, enjoy the sunset, or browse in some shops, instead of dragging in an hour or more after you left the office?

IMPLEMENTATION:

This change requires the involvement of everyone impacted by it. Scheduling several family meetings can be helpful. Consider discussing (1) all that could be gained; (2) the disadvantages or problems; (3) the timing; and (4) the financial impact of selling and buying a home as well as finding adequate schooling for the children.

A CHECKLIST

This chapter presented ten ideas for reducing work time while staying in your current job. Now is the time to examine which ones, if any, are worth pursuing further. Use the chart "Changing the Way I Work" to help you with the process.

CHANGING THE WAY I WORK

Option	Evaluation of its potential			First action step
	Not for me	Has possi- bilities	Act on soon	
Lunchtime personal	___	___	___	___
Reasonable deadlines	___	___	___	___
No to some projects	___	___	___	___
Family as priority	___	___	___	___
Avoid weekend travel	___	___	___	___
Personal appts firm	___	___	___	___
Family on bus. trip	___	___	___	___
Set stop lines	___	___	___	___
Extra vacation time	___	___	___	___
Move closer to work	___	___	___	___

I hope that some of the ten ideas will start you on the path of working less and enjoying life more. It's up to you; no one will do it for you. Since these kinds of work patterns entail risk, try to select one or two that have a chance for success in your organization. Have any of the options, for example, been implemented by your co-workers or others in the organization? Begin slowly and follow the recommendations outlined in Chapter 7.

There are additional ways to downshift. One of these is to *re-structure* your job. This will be the theme of our next chapter.

WHERE WE'VE BEEN / WHERE WE'RE GOING

We have pointed out that if you seek more time for self or family you will need to take the initiative. The chapter presented ten possible changes for managing your workday, all of which could permit you to get your job done and yet shorten or lighten your workweek. While not all of them are likely to be acceptable in your organization, giving a try to one or two could make a difference in your lifestyle. More dramatic options are offered in the next chapter.

Questions for Reflection

1. When I think about making some change in how I work, what troubles me the most? What could I do to reduce the concern?

2. If I make a change, what are some of the benefits I hope to attain?

3. It is often constructive to talk through changes before implementing them. Who would be the best person(s) to talk with?

CHAPTER 6

RISKIER STEPS TOWARD THE LIFE YOU WANT

I love coaching, but anybody can coach.
My wife has just one husband
and my children have just one father.
Some of you may think I'm jumping ship.
I don't believe I'm jumping ship.
I'm diving overboard to save my family.

DANNY AINGE (PRESS CONFERENCE ANNOUNCING HIS
RESIGNATION AS HEAD COACH OF THE PHOENIX SUNS)[1]

CHANGE YOUR WORK ARRANGEMENTS

The last chapter presented downshifting options that focused on how you manage your workday. Here are eight new ideas for restructuring your job so that less time is spent at work.

You will find that these downshifting ideas are riskier, because they represent substantial changes in work patterns and reduce your physical presence onsite. As you can imagine, they are also more difficult to sell. The upside is that they have the potential to yield significantly greater leisure time than the options described earlier.

The possibilities we are going to explore are listed on the following page. They are all designed to help you find more leisure time. We will begin with a look at flextime.

OPTIONS FOR REDUCING WORK TIME

- Arrange for flextime
- Go to a part-time schedule
- Make a lateral or downward move
- Telecommute
- Job share
- Take early or gradual retirement
- Decline promotion
- Create a "portfolio career"

Arrange for Flextime

This option involves working the same total hours per week but in a different configuration. For example, instead of working five days 8 to 5, you work four days 7 to 6. Barbara was able to work out a flextime plan that enabled her to spend more time with her children.

Barbara is a single parent, raising two children: 12-year-old Mark and 14-year-old Beth. Barbara feels uncomfortable about the children's returning from school to an empty house (she herself usually arrives at 5:30). Another problem is the children's transportation. Beth is involved in a gymnastics class and Mark in scouting. Both activities take place some distance from the school and, on many afternoons, arranging the back-and-forth transportation is difficult.

Barbara was able to negotiate an agreement with her boss to work from 6 to 3, instead of the usual 8 to 5. The new hours permit Barbara to arrive home about the same time as her children. She is able to drive them to and from their activities. "What's really great," she said, "is that we have the opportunity to talk about school and their activities. We can share the excitement, and the disappointments, of the moment. It's so different from trying to get them to open up hours later during dinner."

IMPLEMENTATION:

With so many organizations offering flex hours, asking to change working hours is a relatively low-risk request. In order to sell your boss on flextime, you will need to demonstrate that your new work schedule will not impede your effectiveness and how, ideally, it might enhance your productivity. For example, with Barbara's new arrangement (coming in two hours earlier than most of the staff), she was able to assure her boss that she will now have time to assemble up-to-the-minute data for early morning meetings. This data was often needed by her boss, but it was previously unavailable.

Work Part-Time

Here we look at the notion of working a shorter workweek than normal. The range could be from a few hours to several days less per week. This almost always requires a reduction in pay.

Peter is 41 years old and has been an engineer at Hughes Electronics for thirteen years. The company values him for his people skills and innovative technical contributions. However, Peter has a wide range of other interests that he likes to pursue. Peter enjoys the income his Hughes job provides but, as he put it, "I don't want to miss out on all that life has to offer."

Peter hesitated for several years before asking the company to allow him to work three days a week. "It was my own internal resistance," he explained. "I didn't think they would allow it. But, when some rental properties I had started paying off, I was less fearful about income, and I asked the company. After some hesitation, they said OK!"

"It's interesting," he continued, "to discover that my total productivity is as least as good as when I was a working five days. I feel better about the job—it's not such a drag on my life and I no longer have that Sunday evening dread about going back to work on Monday morning."

IMPLEMENTATION:

In selecting this option, be aware that some of your full-time co-workers may feel resentful as you leave on Thursday afternoon. Another risk is that a shorter workweek could result in your being "out of the loop." You may not be there when critical events occur. Ideas for selling your organization on working part time can be found in Chapter 7.

Make a Lateral or Downward Move

Transferring to a less demanding assignment could bring less stress, fewer late evenings, and freer weekends. Such moves are becoming more acceptable in today's organizations and there is lessening disapproval toward someone who makes this choice.

This is a particularly important downshift if you are experiencing feelings of being "in over your head." As many have discovered, long-term persistent job frustration often results in physical and emotional problems. Getting out of the pressure cooker could be a positive step toward better physical and mental health.

Here is John Carlisle's story about a successful downward move. Notice how timing played a key role in selling management on the downshift.

> About five years ago I relocated to take a position as editorial director for a publishing company. The new job was very demanding. I had to rebuild and train much of the editorial staff and, relatively soon after I came on board, the president moved to another firm.
>
> During the search for a replacement, I took on some of the president's responsibilities. From the beginning I was working about 65 hours a week, and then it escalated to 75 and 80. The long hours took their toll on our marriage and on my health.
>
> After about three years, I realized that I was approaching

burnout and needed to negotiate for a demotion. I knew I would be happier as an editor dealing with authors, a pleasurable creative activity and one with fewer responsibilities.

I know that it's risky to tell your company that you want to step down from your position, especially when you're successful in it. But my wife and I agreed that time for us to be together and my health were our top priorities.

I waited for an opening and approached the president at a time when I thought my downshift might benefit the company. I had been interviewing applicants for a newly approved direct-report to me. Within a few weeks we found an ideal candidate, but one who was expressing some doubts about moving his family from New York City.

I proposed a solution: that the candidate be offered *my* job! I sensed that the candidate would probably find the editorial director position more attractive and would agree to move. I told the president that I had reevaluated my work situation and was at a point where I needed to reduce my hours for personal and health reasons, and that I really wanted to return to hands-on editorial work. In addition, I said that we had a candidate who was potentially qualified to do my job.

It took about ten minutes of negotiating to design a new position for me. The job was mine, provided I could successfully recruit the new candidate. When the applicant said yes, it became a win-win for all parties.

For my wife and me there was an initial sense of loss in status and income, but this was more than compensated by the increased time we had together, reduced stress, and the satisfaction of more enjoyable work.[2]

IMPLEMENTATION:
Success in gaining the organization's approval to downshift to a different job or department depends, in large measure, on the following four factors:

1. Your ability to identify, within the organization, a job (or department) that commands less time and energy than your present assignment.

2. The extent to which you have the experience and/or talents to succeed in the new position.

3. The difficulty your boss will have finding your replacement.

4. The willingness of the organization. Acceptance of your proposal depends a lot on the company culture.

Assuming no major problems with these four issues, careful thought must be given to the way you present your request. It is essential that your desire to move out of your present job not be viewed as a sign of weakness or give the appearance that you can't hack it.

It will be important to put a positive spin on your request. One way this can be accomplished is to speak of the move in terms of it being a "developmental step," something that will enhance your value to the organization. For example, you might indicate:

- Your versatility to the company will be enhanced. The new work assignment will require acquisition of additional skills or knowledge that you are eager to acquire.

- The move will enhance your contribution; the new job will tap more fully into certain aptitudes or skills you possess.

- The change will improve new department's productivity. You will bring expertise from your present job that adds to the new group's capability.

Telecommute

Telecommuting means taking advantage of today's personal computers, networking capabilities, e-mail, fax machines, and video/phone conference calls to work at home for one or more days a week. This downshifting option is on the rise. A recent working trends survey by Rutgers University and the University of Connecticut revealed that 8 percent of all workers now telecommute five days a week. An article by Maggie Jackson in the *Portland*

Press Herald reported that 11 million Americans telecommute at least one day a month. Here's a telecommuting example she provided:

> Larry Madsen had to teach his kids to knock at his study door, and he has weaned his neighbors off the idea that they can drop by at all hours. But after seven years of working at home for AT&T, he's a confirmed telecommuter.
>
> "You have to get used to it," said Madsen, a sales manager in suburban Salt Lake City and father of eight. "But I love the freedom of having my office here at home."[3]

Telecommuting will work for you if you have the ability to produce results from afar, are self-disciplined, and have office space. The downside of telecommuting is the possibility of being out of face-to-face contact with company personnel. In most organizations, significant decisions and plans often happen at ad hoc gatherings: a crisis arises and a quick meeting is held, someone stops at a peer's desk to discuss a problem, and staff members have informal opportunities to discuss their accomplishments with their boss.

Successful telecommuting is not easy. It can be lonely without the usual social interactions that occur in most job locations. You will also need to contend with the ordinary distractions of daily life at home.

IMPLEMENTATION:

If telecommuting is commonplace in your organization, gaining approval may not be difficult. Whatever your situation, two selling points need to be mentioned:

1. The ways in which the company will benefit. For example, your telecommuting will free up an office, reduce office overhead, and enhance your productivity (less time spent commuting).

2. Your willingness to be flexible about coming in to the office or plant whenever it is necessary.

When presenting your case, consider alternative telecommuting patterns. For example, starting by telecommuting only one day a week or proposing that you gradually increase the days spent telecommuting over the course of a full year. In some cases, a few days telecommuting may be the best plan to prevent isolation from fellow staff members.

Job Share

This downshifting option involves dividing your job up so that two people perform it. In other words, two individuals share the same job—each working an agreed-upon portion of the week. The key to making this work is the constant sharing of information so that both people are aware of each other's decisions and communication with others.

IMPLEMENTATION:
The difficulty in implementing this option is finding another qualified person who wants to share your job. Many organizations, however, have policies on job sharing and may assist you in recruiting the "other half."

If job sharing is new to your organization, it will take considerable effort to gain approval of the idea. Arlene Hirsch, in her book *Love Your Work and Success Will Follow,* describes the campaign of two working moms—Laura Meier and Loriann Meagher—to sell a job sharing arrangement. Both women were sales managers at Xerox. In part, here is what they did:

> Meier and Meagher drafted a detailed, thirty-page proposal and revised it three times until it adequately addressed the concerns of their immediate boss and the human resources department. In it, they spelled out their schedules, day-to-day tasks, and plans for managing the sales team."[4]

Done properly, job sharing is a downshifting step that can make you look good, so that you are not perceived as less committed. Often it enhances productivity in that the parties bring different strengths to the job.

Take Early or Gradual Retirement

These are options for individuals near retirement age. The opportunity for early retirement comes mostly as a byproduct of downsizing brought on by a company merger or major reorganization. However, in some circumstances early retirement can be pursued on your own. If you are nearing retirement age, you could instigate negotiations about timing and benefits. You will take less retirement income in return for the company's setting an earlier retirement date.

> Dave Ketcher, an investment manager of a large insurance
> company, was offered the choice of an early retirement package or
> relocating to the headquarters of a merger partner. Dave did not
> want to retire, but he took the package. He viewed this event as a
> window of opportunity to move into college teaching, something
> he had always wanted to do. With his financial cushion, Dave was
> able to maintain his usual standard of living despite his low first-
> year teaching salary. His second career put Dave into academia and
> a job in which he thrives.[5]

Another option is to retire gradually by downshifting to shorter days or workweeks, serving as a company consultant, or working on a temporary or seasonal basis. Such arrangements can give you more free time and may be attractive to your firm.

IMPLEMENTATION:

This is an option that requires treading lightly. You don't want the organization to think that you're no longer hard-working and dedicated. It can be the kiss of death if you're perceived as "retired on the job." It would be worthwhile to explore carefully, asking your boss, and then the human resources staff, "How would the company view my taking early [gradual] retirement, *if* I decided to do so?"

Once again, it is vital to be able to explain how the early phase-out could be accomplished with minimal disruption to your work.

You will need to figure out how the job can be managed in fewer hours and/or who can take on some of the work.

Refuse Some Promotions

This downshift involves declining a promotion that will result in heavier workloads or an undesired relocation. The risk is that you may be perceived as not being a team player or as lacking ambition. However, in most organizations, your first refusal is minimally risky—especially if your explanation is predicated on family needs. It is usually the second and third refusals that limit being asked again.

IMPLEMENTATION:

Promotions are tempting. They often bring with them increased control, more income, and greater status—goodies the world would have us believe bring happiness. While nice, they don't necessarily equate with happiness. You need to weigh these temptations against the joy of closer relationships, more personal freedom, your family's wishes, and your health.

When turning down a promotion offer, be careful that you do not convey a low level of ambition, or limited support for the organization. You can avoid this danger by mentioning whichever of the following points are valid for you:

1. You like the organization.
2. You are very satisfied with your present job and how well it taps into your abilities.
3. You are flattered by the offer and believe you could do the job.
4. Right now, the promotion would be "too disruptive for your family and its needs."
5. You would be interested, at another time, in this or other promotional opportunities.

Create a Portfolio Career

Portfolio career is a relatively new term. *Los Angeles Times* writer, Donns K.H. Walters described the portfolio career as a work arrangement in which an individual has "a mixture of part-time jobs or a combination of part-time with temporary, contract, freelance, consulting, or self-employment."[6] Ginny Miller is an example of someone pursuing a portfolio career:

> Ginny works part-time in her town library, writes the social column for her local newspaper, and works at home as an indexer for a New York publisher.

One advantage of a portfolio career is that it enables you to use your talents in a variety of settings. Another is flexibility. Walters reported the story of Allyne Sitkoff Lewis, a Los Angeles woman, who chose the portfolio way of working.

> Allyne works part-time as a receptionist in a medical office and teaches at a nursery school. She enjoys the flexibility, and said "Being able to work with both adults and children is nice."
>
> And, unlike the way it was when her own children were growing up and finances were tighter, she now can set her own work pace. When she felt like slowing down recently, she switched to substituting at the nursery school.

A third advantage of a portfolio career is greater job security. If one source of income is lost, you still have others to fall back upon. All of your emotional and financial security isn't tied up in one job. The downside is probable loss of benefits that come with full-time employment.

IMPLEMENTATION:

A beginning step is to determine how much you want to work and the talents you want to employ. You then need to search the marketplace for the work settings that will provide the income and variety you want. When these are accomplished, you can approach your employer about working on a part-time basis. Suggestions for gaining your organization's approval were described in the Working Part-time section of this chapter.

A CHECKLIST

I have provided eight possible ways to restructure your job so that less time is spent at work. Look at the accompanying list to determine which, if any, are worth your pursuing further.

SPENDING LESS TIME AT WORK

Option	Evaluation of its potential			First action step
	Not for me	*Has possibilities*	*Act on soon*	
Flextime	___	___	___	___
Work Part-time	___	___	___	___
Telecommute	___	___	___	___
Job share	___	___	___	___
Early/gradual retirement	___	___	___	___
Lateral/downward move	___	___	___	___
Decline promotion	___	___	___	___
Portfolio career	___	___	___	___

Combining Options

You may want to consider combining two or more options. For example, you might blend part-time work and telecommuting or downshift to a less demanding job or department that is amenable to flextime. In Chapter 5, we mentioned ten low-risk ways to downshift. These could also be blended with the riskier moves of this chapter.

WHERE WE'VE BEEN / WHERE WE'RE GOING

If you are serious about wanting more time for yourself and your loved ones, a significant change in work patterns is usually necessary. This chapter provided eight work-changing options, all of which involve significant risk. The upside is that they have great potential for helping you to change your lifestyle. It really comes down to the question of how badly you want more time. Examples presented individuals who took the bold steps because they decided that, for them, the gains were greater than the risks.

If you are ready to move on, to take some action steps, the next chapter will be interesting. It presents an overall game plan for getting your organization to agree to your plans for downshifting.

Questions for Reflection

1. On average, how much time per week would I like to carve away from my work?

2. Of the eight options presented in this chapter, which ones (if any) struck a positive note—perhaps leading me to think "I'd like to try that"? Reflecting on that, what feelings do I have? Scared? Excited? Warm? What?

3. When would be the best time to begin efforts at downshifting? What are my risks in delaying?

CHAPTER 7

GETTING YOUR ORGANIZATION'S BUY-IN

Control your destiny or someone else will.

Jack Welch[1], CEO, General Electric

DEFUSING POTENTIAL RESISTANCE

Before you begin this chapter, please allow me to slip in a quick "Congratulations!" The greeting is in order because, if you are reading this chapter, you have no doubt made a psychological turn. You've made a decision to do something about bettering your life—a desire many dream about, but few act upon.

Successful salespersons tell us that the key to making a sale is to win your customer's trust and confidence. The same is true for downshifting. In this case, the customer is your organization, and in particular, your boss. While you may work in a company that supports *some* downshifting activities (such as flextime or telecommuting), to win company approval for your particular plan will require effort on your part.

This chapter presents guidelines for gaining organizational support for your downshifting plan. All of the suggestions embrace sound marketing principles, but, of course, may not fit every circumstance. Your judicious application of these recommendations will significantly enhance the likelihood of "making the sale." Let's look at them.

Know What You Really Want

A wishy-washy presentation makes everyone uncomfortable and is almost always ineffective. It is essential that you be clear in your own mind about exactly what you want to do and how it will play out on the job. If you are torn between two or more downshifting choices, go back to the drawing board and try to narrow the focus. You may find it helpful to enlist your family or friends in working through the pros and cons before arriving at your final decision. Your objective is to come across to management as confident and clear about your downshifting desires.

Make Your Boss A Friend

For almost all downshifting steps, you will need your manager's support. If you and your boss already have a close, trusting relationship, that is great. If not, you need to begin gaining your manager's favor. Some effective ways to do this are:

- Initiate new avenues of communication. Find ways to talk with your manager about your work, especially when you're making good progress. On the other hand, if the job isn't going well, initiate a discussion about your concerns and desire to improve. Ask for your manager's input.

- Volunteer to take on a project or assignment that needs doing. Do not make this offer, however, if your usual responsibilities will suffer as a consequence.

Another way to increase the probability of winning your boss's approval is take a tip from successful salespeople and pre-sell your downshifting desire. The idea is to mention the possibility of cutting back, but in such a way that it does not alarm your boss. You would like the idea of downshifting to become familiar, so that when you make your actual request, it will not come as a surprise. Any initial resistance can be defused in this way. For example:

> "I have to do something different, I haven't been home for dinner once this week." Or "One of these days, I'd love to find a way to get some longer weekends."

Put It in Writing

Eventually your manager will have to present your request up the line. Even if you have the support of your boss, ammunition will be needed to convince others. For this reason, it is essential, especially with the high-risk options, that you submit a written proposal. It should be written with the same style and objectivity as a capital expense request or a sales proposal. Here are a few ideas for preparing it:

1. *Be specific about what you want to do.* Include the way your work schedule will change, precisely what hours/days you will work, how you will interface with co-workers, and so on.

2. *Describe how the new arrangement will enable you (or designated others) to meet your performance goals.* **This is essential!** Most likely, this will be your boss's prime concern. Your write-up should be specific and, if possible, discuss all contingencies.

3. *Show how the new work arrangement will benefit the company.* In a section entitled, "Advantages for the Organization," include, if possible, how your downshifting will:

    • Reduce company costs (for example, lower salary, some duties assigned to lower-paid assistant, lower overhead (office space, equipment use, etc.)

    • Yield greater productivity (for example, less fatigue and hence more creativity, less commuting time and hence more time available for work projects, etc.)

    • Create higher morale (for example, you'll be happier, even more committed to the company, want to build your future here; be careful that you don't imply you're not fully dedicated right now!)

4. *State clearly how you envision your salary would be altered or prorated in light of your new work schedule.*

Tap into Your Support Network

There may be others in your organization (your human resources staff, for example) that will need to be brought on board. Are there influential persons you know in the organization who could advocate for you or be supportive, should their opinion be solicited? It would be helpful to talk with such individuals confidentially. Ask about their reactions to your idea and how they would be willing to help.

Highlight Your Flexibility

You need to be explicit about your willingness to adapt to company needs. Your boss has to feel confident that, in peak times or crises, you'll be available; they can still count on you (as long as the crises aren't weekly!). It is important, of course, to monitor your accommodations so that they don't become the new norm.

Your willingness to put aside your reduced/changed work schedule temporarily to accommodate the company is often the factor that gains approval for your downshifting idea.

Another way to demonstrate your flexibility is to offer to downshift on a trial basis. This offer is particularly helpful should you encounter resistance to your plan. An example comes from an article in *Health* magazine, in which Edward Dolnick describes how:

> Suzanne Nanix and Charlotte Schutzman concocted a plan for how they would share a job (each working half-time) at Bell Atlantic. They proposed a six-month trial period. "We told them we'd agree it wasn't working if anybody had to tell either one of us the same thing twice," says Nanix. The two have job shared for five years—and through four promotions.[2]

DO YOUR HOMEWORK

Investigate HR Policies and Practices

Many organizations have written policies about flextime, telecommuting, vacation time, or job sharing. If the organization's policies are supportive of your downshifting desire, you can cite them when making your request. If they are not supportive, at least you will be aware of potential policy barriers. Also be aware that company practices may differ from written policy. Check around the organization to see how others have downshifted. You may find precedence for your request.

Anticipate Your Manager's Objections

Even if you make a strong and positive presentation, objections are likely to arise. While you can't anticipate all of them, some are predictable. Here are a few examples cited by Dolnick:

- "What does this say about your commitment to your job?"
  Response: Instead of focusing exclusively on your personal reasons for wanting to downshift, talk up your professional goals and how the change may enhance your efforts at continued development.

- "Everyone will want to do it."
  Response: Point out that not everyone wants or can afford to work less time.

- What will your staff or coworkers do on your days off?"
  Response: Explain that you will stay in touch by the company's computer network, phone, or fax, just as you do now when you're out of the office.

While it is helpful to have some answers ready for anticipated objections, don't fall into the trap of responding quickly with your prepared answers. Instead, listen carefully, ask questions, and clarify all objections. For example:

Boss: If you're gone for four weeks, a lot of problems could come up that would need your involvement. We couldn't wait until you got back.

> *You:*   You're hesitant to approve my taking two extra weeks' vaca-
>   tion because you're concerned that problems may come up
>   that no one else can handle.

or

> *Boss:*   I don't think that human resources would go along with
>   your plan.
>
> *You:*   You're not so sure it can be sold up the line.

Paraphrasing objections keeps you from arguing and, perhaps even more important, helps your boss view an objection from a fresh perspective. When you paraphrase your manager's objections, you create a discussion climate that often leads to problem solving. In turn, this develops an atmosphere that increases the probability of your getting a yes.

Have a "Plan B"

Suppose you run into a stone wall and your boss flat out says no? Instead of walking away thinking this is the end of it, have in mind a next step you can propose, something that will keep your downshifting proposal alive. For example:

> "I understand why you're not positive about my downshifting
> idea. If it's all right with you, I'd like to think about it and address
> the issues you raised. Maybe I could find some adjustments to
> make it more palatable. Can we talk about it a little more next
> week, perhaps this same time next Friday?"

Even if you can't think of any significant adjustments that will still keep the downshifting palatable, make some minor modifications just to keep the proposal alive. Your willingness to consider your boss's objections counts a lot; it creates a climate for further discussion in which your manager might be more receptive.

The main point is, if all goes badly, try not to leave as though the issue were dead. Pave the way for a second pass. As Yogi Berra said, "It's not over till it's over."

WHERE WE'VE BEEN / WHERE WE'RE GOING

This chapter pointed out the importance of preparing your case by developing a business-like proposal for presenting your downshifting request. In your presentation, you will need to demonstrate that your downshifting will not impact negatively on performance goals. Another part of the proposal should explain, in positive terms, how the company will benefit from your downshift. We pointed out, too, the crucial importance of gaining your manager's support as well as the support of trusted friends within your organization.

When you encounter objections to your plan, listen and, instead of arguing, try to paraphrase the objection. This creates a more relaxed climate, one that fosters give-and-take discussion.

What if all goes wrong? What if they say no? That's the topic we'll explore in the next chapter.

Questions for Reflection

1. How do I want to downshift? How clear and precisely defined is my plan? If it seems sketchy or ambiguous, how can I better spell it out?

2. What objections is my boss most likely to raise?

3. With whom in the company would it be valuable for me to discuss, on a confidential basis, my downshifting plans?

4. If I had to come up with "Plan B," what would it be?

CHAPTER 8

WHEN THE ANSWER IS NO

Don't ever slam a door; you might want to go back.
DON HEROLD[1]

SHOT DOWN—NOW WHAT?

If you are reading this chapter, you may be anticipating difficulty in selling your plan to downshift or perhaps it has already been shot down. So now you're facing a critical decision—what to do next. For most of us, three options are available:

1. Stay put
2. Try again
3. Leave

We'll discuss each of these alternatives to help you arrive at a decision. However, even though we review the pros and cons of each alternative, the overriding consideration for you is "How important is it to me that I change my lifestyle?" We'll talk more about this. Now let's turn to your first option.

Stay Put

As you can imagine, there are some potent negatives to this option. One downside of staying put is the possibility of a psychological setback. As with any loss, you may experience a diminishment of enthusiasm or self-confidence. After all, staying put represents giving up, at least temporarily, your hopes for a better life for you and your loved ones.

Another problem with staying put is that once again you are placing yourself in the hands of others. Instead of taking charge of your life, you will be adopting a passive role. How does that sit with you? If you do nothing (stay put), you may temporarily experience reduced discomfort because what is familiar seems safe, but later on regret and depression are likely. In any event, staying put means that you will not enjoy the exhilarating feeling that accompanies taking control of your life.

A third problem with staying put is that you remain in the frying pan. You will still be suffering from the same pressures—the same lack of time for family or your personal life—that led you to consider downshifting in the first place.

Susan Arledge, an experienced outplacement counselor in Portland, Maine, encountered a strong temptation to stick with status quo. Here's what she told me:

> To think about downshifting is one thing, but to actually do it
> is quite another. I knew it was time for me to move on, but loyalty
> to my business partners got in the way, along with the close rela-
> tionships I had with the office staff. I have to admit, too, that our
> gorgeous office overlooking the water kept me there longer than
> was necessary.
>
> I didn't downshift within my company. . . [I] left and stayed in
> the same career, but not in a situation that was competitive to my
> prior employer. The impetus for leaving was to devote time to the
> passion I have for motivational speaking. I needed a calmer atmo-
> sphere in which to develop the talks, so I got a two-day-a-week

consulting job, aligned with my passion for career development and diversity issues, to support my "speaking addiction." I now have time to spend hours online and in libraries working on my speeches.

What I have found is a renewed sense of purpose, with time for my family, volunteer work, and long lunches with friends. I feel so much more energized and, at the same time, centered. It was the best decision I have made in many years.[2]

It's often tempting to stay put because change itself is anxiety provoking. We justify standing pat because even if we don't like our current work demands, we know what we're dealing with. Moreover, sometimes people remain in unhealthy situations because they hope that things will change. No doubt the company will change, but it could be for the worse! Staying put for this reason is not likely to get you off the treadmill.

On the other hand, if you know of an impending organizational change (merger with a more flexible organization, new boss, new HR manager) that might result in your downshifting proposal being viewed more positively, it may be prudent to hang in there for awhile. In such cases, set a reasonable target date. If the change doesn't occur by your deadline, consider the two options that follow.

Try Again

A factor to consider when making your decisions about trying again is the extent of negativity you encountered. If the rejection was a categorical no, perhaps tinged with angry overtones, trying again could result in ongoing resentment or even put your job in jeopardy. It depends on the organization's culture and your boss's personality.

On the other hand, if you've had it with the job, trying again may not result in your losing much. The worst is that you may have to leave. The upside is that, if you persist, you may create the possibility for approval of your downshifting request.

When making a second pass to sell your downshifting idea, success is usually dependent upon your ability *to present a new alternative*. Even if it is only a slight variation of the original, it can open the door to another chance. Your willingness to seek an acceptable option creates a positive discussion climate because it shows respect for your boss's opinion.

The basic sources for your options are:

1. *The nature of the downshift: Propose a different way of downshifting.* For example: "If you don't think my job sharing arrangement is feasible, would you consider, instead, letting me work four days a week?"

    Ideally, explain how your new alternative minimizes or overcomes the problems raised during your initial presentation. For instance: "You were concerned that telecommuting four days a week will result in my being absent from important meetings. Suppose I agreed to come to the office for these meetings, even though they occur on days I'm working at home. I only live 25 minutes away, and if needed, I could be here on short notice."

2. *Timing: Offer to Change the scheduling.* For example: "Suppose I put off downshifting until the end of next quarter when we start hiring our summer interns?"

Finally, consider how you'll feel about yourself if you don't give your downshifting request your best shot. You may spend a long time wondering how it might have been if you tried a little harder. On the other hand, if you've made an all-out effort and no meaningful progress is evident, it may be time to consider seeking a different place to work.

Leave the Organization

There comes a time when enough is enough. There is a point at which you conclude that your happiness and the happiness of those you love is too important to defer. If this is your sentiment, it's time to remove yourself from an unhealthy situation. However, quitting the organization is often a traumatic move. It feels safer to stay put.

One way to get over the decision-to-quit hurdle is to accept the fact that no job is safe. Richard Leider and David Shapiro, in *Repacking Your Bags*, put it this way:

> The idea of a permanent job is obsolete. . . . The work world is in constant turmoil. Once-powerful businesses teeter on the brink of extinction. Companies whose names used to be synonymous with security are laying people off in record numbers. Your job may disappear out from under you at any moment without warning. These days, nearly everyone will be "between jobs" at some time.[3]

Before you take any action, discuss your intentions with those you love, the people who will be most impacted by your action. Keep them informed and involve them in the what-if planning. A wonderful ancillary benefit from these discussions is increased closeness and strengthened relationships. You may also be surprised at the number of constructive ideas your loved ones offer for easing the transition to a new job.

Another wise move at this point is to talk with a career counselor. Such a professional can help you examine your values, interests, skills, and preferred work setting, plus the number of hours per week you want to devote to work. A counselor can also help save time and energy in determining the career path that best meets your needs.

If you've made the decision to leave, here are some suggestions for making your departure in a professional (and minimally risky) manner:

1. *Start looking for a new position early on.* The best of all worlds is having a new job already lined up that better suits your desired lifestyle. Short of that, begin a quiet job campaign so that you aren't postponing the employment searching process until after you've left. The risk here is that the organization may prematurely learn of your job search.

2. *Talk with your boss first.* If your manager hears via office gossip or the rumor mill that you're planning to leave, it is likely to

engender bad feelings. This is a bridge you don't need to burn. There is also the possibility your boss will make a counteroffer that meets your downshifting needs. Consider too that, should you change your mind and stay, it might be a bit awkward to face the co-workers you prematurely told about your plans to leave.

In preparation for this meeting, plan a simple speech. Don't spend time trying to gently lead up to the point. Be brief and get your intention out on the table. Basically, you should mention:

- Your intention to leave

- Your planned date of departure

- Ways you are willing to ease the departure (train substitute, change timing)

- Your gratitude for the opportunity to work at the present organization, and (only if it's true) your enjoyment in working with your boss

Notice that no mention is made of the reasons you are resigning. It is best to keep them in reserve until you are asked why. Then, be prepared to explain calmly and concisely the organization's unwillingness for you to downshift.

3. *Give sufficient notice.* You might avoid a confrontation by departing for good on a Friday afternoon without saying anything, but you would pay a high price for it (potential benefits losses, poor references, networking losses, and more). Rather, give your organization two weeks' notice—more if you're one of the firm's top executives.

4. *Put your resignation in writing.* After you've verbally presented your notice, address a brief letter to your boss. In this way, you can be certain that your words are accurately communicated. Simply state your intention to resign and designate the last day of your employment. Do not mention your reasons for departing. In wording the letter, keep in mind that it will end up in your permanent employee record.

5. *Get your finances organized.* Unless you already have a new job lined up, it is prudent to make contingency plans. How long can you last without income? What can you do without? What can you sell, if need be? Where could you borrow money, if necessary? Consider getting a loan application approved (home equity, for instance) while you're still working.

6. *Ease the departure.* The idea is to leave management with a positive view of your leaving. You can help achieve this goal by offering to:

- Train your replacement

- Delay your departure (a reasonable amount of time) until a replacement is found

- Tie up unfinished projects so that an orderly transition occurs

- Make yourself available by phone for a few weeks after your departure, should problems arise

- Serve as a consultant for short periods of time (wonderful income source if you don't have another job lined up)

   Your goal here is to avoid burning bridges by helping the organization fill the void your absence creates. At the same time, it may aid you in negotiating a better severance arrangement.

7. *Negotiate with human resources.* A meeting with HR staff is standard procedure in almost all organizations. It usually involves return of company property (keys, credit cards, company access cards) and making arrangements for benefits to be transferred or terminated. In the area of benefit termination, some negotiation is often possible. At stake here are the duration that health and life insurance will remain in force as well as the amount, procedure, and timing of the distribution of bonus, profit sharing, and retirement monies. Before your meeting, informally determine which benefit items have been negotiated in the past and plan your strategies accordingly. You don't have to accept the first arrangement that HR lays out. In ambiguous situations, consultation with a lawyer could prove helpful.

8. *Line up references.* If you will be seeking new employment, you will need references. The best time to ask co-workers to serve as references is *before* you depart the premises. Face-to-face discussions make it easier for others to be supportive because you can readily explain your reasons for leaving and what you hope the future holds.

9. *Depart on an upbeat note.* You never know when you may need help from the organization. Leave with good words about the organization and its staff.

IN THE FINAL ANALYSIS

Making your choice between staying put, trying again, and leaving may come easily if the path is clear and you feel confident about your decision. In such instances, all that needs to be done is to select your timing and make plans to put your decision into action.

On the other hand, you may feel uncertain about the direction to take. To help resolve the doubts, pay attention to your gut instincts. These unvoiced vibes do not materialize from nowhere; they are input worth considering because they evolve from subtle, unrecognized cues or unconscious thoughts. If you are undecided between two options, ask yourself "What feels right?"

Ultimately, it comes down to how badly you want to change your lifestyle. Only you can answer this question, but feedback from friends and loved ones can help you reach the right conclusion. Chapter 10 may also prove helpful in making your decision.

WHERE WE'VE BEEN / WHERE WE'RE GOING

When your boss says no to your request to downshift, three options are available: stay put, try again, or leave. The correct choice depends upon the extent of the job discomfort you are currently experiencing, how bad you'll feel if you give up the idea of downshifting, and the likelihood that a second sales effort will win management approval. We pointed out that if you are truly "on the fence," discussing the pros and cons with friends and family (and reading Chapter 10) could be beneficial.

We also provided a list of constructive steps for leaving the organization. The importance of parting company on an upbeat note, not burning your bridges, was highlighted.

The next chapter will bring a smile to your face. It shares with you ways to make your downshifting pay off. You will learn how best to use your new-found time to bring more happiness into your life and the lives of those you care most about.

Questions for Reflection

1. If I am undecided about my next step, who would be the best person with whom to discuss it?

2. How could I re-approach my boss with a slightly different downshifting plan? What new objections, if any, are likely to be raised?

3. Suppose I decide to quit, what's the worst that can happen? How could I minimize the downside?

CHAPTER 9

YOU DID IT!

Take away love and our earth is a tomb.
Robert Browning[1]

CONSCIOUSLY CREATING HAPPINESS

If your downshifting process is underway, great! But have you thought about the best ways to make use of your newfound time? Even if you already have an agenda, reading this chapter can help you avoid false starts and steer you in the best directions. It might be interesting, as well, to compare the results of current psychological research on personal satisfaction with your own life experiences.

Some selected findings about happiness will be described here. Even if you never downshift, acting on these findings has the potential to bring greater happiness into your life. We begin by pointing out action steps you might be tempted to take, but which do not lead to increased happiness.

Some Traps to Avoid

1. *You don't get happy by simply deciding to get rid of unhappiness.*
    Conventional wisdom is that if we eliminate the things in our
    lives that make us unhappy we'll be happier. Unfortunately it
    doesn't work that way. Researchers are discovering that happiness
    and unhappiness are feelings that coexist and can rise and fall in-
    dependently, much as with love and hate in close relationships.
    Changes in one don't necessarily effect changes in the other.

    It is true, of course, that getting rid of things that cause us un-
    happiness can reduce our level of discontent. Getting out of a
    painful relationship, for example, can significantly reduce your
    discomfort, but it won't make you happy. If you want happiness,
    you'll have to take some *positive* steps. You might, for example,
    become more actively involved in church or community activi-
    ties or begin establishing a new relationship.

2. *You don't get happy by pursuing the three P's: power, possessions, and
    prestige.* Sooner or later, life experience tells us that happiness
    does not come from chasing after the three P's. The myth is that
    when you get to be VP, or score the corner office, or a buy a big-
    ger house, or land that BMW, it will bring you happiness. It's
    only when we get there that we discover there are others with
    more of what we just attained, and that our initial burst of satis-
    faction is short-lived. If you want to cut to the chase, avoid
    spending newfound time seeking happiness from things or even
    people, and recognize that happiness comes from within. We'll
    focus more on this later as we discuss relationships.

3. *You don't get happy through more wealth or job advancement.* If you
    have downshifted, no doubt you already know that money and
    jobs are not stepping-stones to happiness. Psychological research
    supports your conclusion. There is little positive correlation be-
    tween happiness and income or job level. On the average, top ex-
    ecutives aren't any happier than their secretaries. It's OK to earn
    more or to advance, but investing time to pursue either one is
    not likely to bring increased happiness.

Some Paths to Fulfillment

In this section we'll shift the focus and examine what psychologists
say does bring happiness into our lives. Interestingly enough,

happy people have common characteristics, so by examining their experiences we can determine which ones might profitably be applied to how we live. Check out the list of factors common to happy people, which we will now discuss one by one.

FACTORS COMMON TO HAPPY PEOPLE

1. Engage in activities they enjoy
2. Reach out to others
3. Maintain good health
4. Seek peace and comfort in spirituality
5. Have at least one close, intimate relationship

1. *Happy people engage in activities they enjoy.* Whether at work or play, happy people report that they "do things they like to do." Psychological research also reveals that the more often you engage in activities you enjoy the happier you're likely to be. If downshifting has given you more free time, one option to consider is to engage more often in whatever brings you satisfaction. If you enjoy

- Oil painting, paint more often

- Playing with your children, play more often

- Reading, read more often

- Walking, walk more often

The same concept applies to work. Your cutting back may free you to search out the job that involves more activities that you enjoy. Here's a typical example:

> Tom Himple served as principal of a large suburban high school for six years. He was superb in this role, earning respect from faculty, students, and parents. No small feat! During his tenure, the high school was also designated by the Department of Education as a School of Excellence.

But, Tom wasn't enjoying being principal. He missed the hands-on contact with students and the process of teaching. As a teacher, he enjoyed the challenge of inspiring the uninspired student and the satisfaction from seeing students "get it" after being confronted with a difficult concept.

Last year, Tom resigned as principal and resumed teaching in the same high school. He now takes home less pay but, as he put it, "I go home each day with a smile on my face."[2]

2. *Happy people get involved in helping others.* There is no need to describe how happiness floods us when we reach out to someone in need. We've all experienced it. One helpful principle in reaching out is to choose situations that you find satisfying and/or for which you have talent. If, for example, you are involved in a community project, join a committee that taps into your natural skills. If you have a flair for writing, volunteer to help with the newsletter; don't get trapped into becoming a campaign solicitor (unless, of course, that is something you enjoy doing).

> Andy Basset, a retired boat builder, has a wonderful talent for playing the piano. One day each week he plays at two local nursing homes as well as for most senior citizen events. All seem to enjoy his playing and, as he put it, "Where else could I have so much fun?"

For most of us, opportunities to help abound in our families: a young couple needs a babysitter so they can have a night out, a relative in a nursing home needs someone to chat with, a college-bound cousin needs financial help or tutoring, a brother or sister needs to be forgiven (or from whom forgiveness should be sought). If downshifting provides you with more leisure time, more frequent reaching out can be wonderfully rewarding.

3. *Happy people maintain good health.* It's difficult to feel happy when you are not feeling well. Even a mild toothache makes us "scratchy." This finding highlights the importance of investing some of your newfound time in better health care such as more exercise, balanced diet, and regular checkups.

Good health involves our psyche as well as our body. Often we are so caught up in our busyness that we put off dealing with troubling problems or issues. They can drag us down, sometimes resulting in tension, depression, or psychosomatic symptoms (migraine headaches, colitis, high blood pressure). With more free time, worries and concerns can more readily be addressed. Investing time with a professional counselor can save much time and energy. Such a person can help you sort through the issues and help evolve a constructive plan for coping with your concerns.

4. *Happy people seek peace and comfort in spirituality.* I shall be using the word God interchangeably with Higher Power or Source or Higher Being. You define God in whatever way is meaningful for you. Discussion of spirituality often raises strong emotions— some positive and some decidedly negative. You have a right to your own beliefs, and I'm not suggesting you change them. It is interesting, though, to note that belief in a "higher being" is far more common among happy persons than among non-believers.

One reason that spiritual people tend to be happier is they accept that they don't have all the answers. They can seek consolation and help beyond themselves, so that they are often able to face difficulties or even tragedy with peace and inner strength.

People with a spiritual life may be happy because their faith provides purpose and meaning to life. When spirituality is expressed through religious practice, many find support in their community of believers and direction from the religion's espoused values. They feel comfortable in knowing a "right path" in guiding their decisions and actions.

A variety of medical research studies (*Newsweek*, June 14, 1999) demonstrate how belief in a higher power promotes health and speeds up healing. For example, the American Heart Association, in their Pressure Point advertising series, described a study of 112 women that "found a direct relationship between strong religious belief and low blood pressure that was independent of other health-related behaviors."[3]

If you want to make better use of spiritual resources, here are a few suggestions. However, before we discuss avenues to spirituality, it is helpful to take a look at some common obstacles. If any of these barriers are part of your makeup, you'll need to over-come them. There are a host of external obstacles to spiritual growth, including peer pressure, negative experiences of religion, and preoccupation with daily life. But the most significant obstacle is internal; it is your ego.

To place faith in a power greater than yourself means accepting that you don't have control over your life, that you recognize the need to call on a higher being for help and for answers that you cannot provide. To the degree that you are egocentric, spirituality becomes difficult.

Another obstacle is lack of trust. If you have faith, you can place your problems before God and trust that you will be heard. Many individuals don't trust anyone, not even their spouses or parents. Such persons will find it difficult to place their trust in a Higher Being. To enhance your spirituality:

• *Make time for reflection.* People with strong spirituality often report a deepening of faith when meditating, reading, or attending weekend retreats. Quiet time, in solitude, is conducive to spiritual growth.

• *Promise yourself to open up to spiritual growth.* It is important to make this decision consciously. One way to translate this promise into action is to refrain from arguing (either silently or with others) when someone speaks about religion or spiritual matters. Instead, listen and try to understand what they believe and why. Speak with others you know who are involved in church or on a faith journey or spiritual path.

• *Look for your Source in the beauties of Nature.* Give yourself time to reflect on the wonderment of creation. Many people, for example, become more aware of their finite nature and human limitations as they stargaze on a clear night and look in awe at the order and vastness of space.

• *Join a religious organization.* Being with others who espouse faith is affirming. Comments by religious leaders often can be inspiring and encourage greater spirituality.

• *Pray for increased faith.* Express your desire for increased trust in a Higher Being. Pray about your fears, hopes, and desires.

Spiritual awakening many times accompanies a mid-life or personal crisis. At those times it can be almost instantaneous. However, more often than not, faith evolves from increased openness to such a relationship. It took St. Augustine thirty years of detours before he came to the conclusion that "our hearts were made for you, oh God, and they shall not rest until they rest in Thee."[4]

5. *Happy people nurture, or develop, at least one intimate relationship.* Among the studies of happy individuals, this finding is the most universal. It is so important to your happiness that the remainder of this chapter is devoted to discussing how and why a major portion of any newfound time should be allocated to building closer relationships with those you care most about. Your most intimate relationships could be with your spouse, partner, child, friend, relative, or significant other.

BUILDING CLOSER RELATIONSHIPS

Why We Need Intimacy

It is natural to seek close relationships with others. As humans we are naturally social, even though this trait is sometimes hidden by shyness or insecurity. The perpetuation of our species requires nurturing care through infancy and childhood. It is clearly established that infants thrive (and survive) best in a loving environment—one that includes much holding, touching, and gentle verbal interaction. These needs are not diminished when we become adult. *Our need for intimacy never leaves us.*

This can be readily understood when we recognize that the opposite of intimacy is loneliness. You have probably experienced small doses of this whenever you felt hurt by something a loved one said or did. At those moments you probably acted cool and aloof from your partner, making a distance clearly evident. Perhaps you then tried to replace the emptiness with work activities, or sports, or your hobby—something to take your mind off the pain of the separation. But these diversions work only briefly. We need closeness, and even though we are busy the ache of loneliness remains.

Rewards of Intimacy

Happy individuals have this to say about the rewards of intimate relationships. They:

- Give meaning and purpose to life
- Enhance joy when success is experienced
- Provide support in times of trouble
- Shape a more positive self-image and enhance self-esteem
- Provide a source of deep personal satisfaction by fulfilling their need to love and be loved.

In a nutshell, happy people indicate that close relationships make life worth living.

Peter Jones put it well: "Love doesn't make the world go 'round. Love is what makes the ride worthwhile." Given the potential that close relationships have for bringing deep satisfaction in our lives, why do so many of us put our priorities elsewhere?

Obstacles to Intimacy

At some time or another, most of us either overlook or dismiss the happiness-producing potential of close relationships. For some, it's a matter of timing. Their need to "make it" results in a disproportionate amount of time devoted to career. They believe they will make themselves more available for family and relationships after certain financial goals are achieved. For others, dysfunctional family backgrounds have shown them that close relationships are likely to lead to hurt or pain. They fear being hurt because they have experienced the pain of rejection or separation from a spouse, close partner, child, or relative.

At other times, fear arises from the failure of some relationship in the past. The memory of that pain results in the building of "walls" to keep others from getting close. These folks figuratively hang a "Do Not Disturb" sign around their necks.

Some people have learned to seek personal satisfaction only from their achievements at work or play. As a consequence, they rarely view the development of relationships as an important source of happiness. Still others find their need for security linked to income or money in the bank. Their time and attention are so focused on accumulating wealth that relationship-building gets little attention.

Do any of these reasons hold you back from enjoying the benefits of a closer love relationship? This might be an appropriate time to take stock on this key issue. Check out "What Gets in the Way of My Building Closer Relationships?" for a list of factors that most often get in the way of relationships and note all of those that apply to you.

WHAT GETS IN THE WAY OF MY BUILDING CLOSER RELATIONSHIPS?

	Yes	Somewhat	No
Too busy			
Dysfunctional family background			
Fear of being hurt			
Memories of failures in past relationships			
Primarily seek satisfaction from achievements			
Need for financial security			

This may be an appropriate time for you to look at your close relationships. An easy starting point is to list the persons for whom you care the most, and then note the amount of time and attention you allocate to them. "Analyzing My Time Allocation to Loved Ones" provides a handy format that allows you to begin planning ways to be more present to those you love.

ANALYZING MY TIME ALLOCATION TO LOVED ONES

Name	My Time & Attention			Possible Action
	Not enough	*Right amount*	*Too much*	
Example:				
Susie	X			*Drive to soccer pract.*

BUILDING BLOCKS TO CLOSER RELATIONSHIPS

There is no secret about what is required to build and maintain a close relationship. The basics are simple. Both parties must:

1. Trust each other
2. Give sufficient time to the relationship
3. Alter their sense of privacy
4. Be supportive

Trust

Trust is the bedrock, the stuff upon which all good relationships are built. Without it, relationships collapse. Trust is something that has to be earned, and this takes time because trust derives from our behavior, not our words. We earn trust by demonstrating honesty, predictability, and dependability.

1. *Honesty.* It is almost impossible to trust someone who only tells half-truths or leaves out part of the story. We trust those who "tell it like it is." We may not always like what we hear, but we believe that what we're told accurately reflects their thoughts or feelings. In close relationships, honesty is most meaningfully conveyed by open communication in which we say what we mean and mean what we say. We need to be straightforward about situations and events, but even more so about ourselves and what is going on inside us. We'll talk more about this later.

2. *Predictability.* This is important because predictability helps create a climate conducive to open sharing. Without such sharing, little closeness is possible. It goes like this: If partners can't predict how we will react (at least most of the time) they will feel inhibited about sharing their thoughts or feelings—especially if they are "touchy" or sensitive. Linda and Tom are a case in point:

   > Linda and Tom have been dating for nearly six months. The easy give and take of their conversation led them both to talk about hopes and dreams and other such things that lovers share. Last week, during a relaxed conversation, Linda told Tom about her fear of heights. To her surprise, he laughed at her, saying "It's all in your mind, shake it off."
   >
   > Linda was shocked. This reaction was so different from Tom's previous responses and seeming acceptance of her. His unpredicted behavior shook her deeply. She realized that now she would need to be more guarded about what she revealed to Tom.

3. *Dependability.* Within the context of a relationship, dependability means that you do what you say you will do. It's hard to trust

someone if you can't count on them. If your partner says she will pick up Johnny at school, but then doesn't, you may excuse the behavior. But if it happens a second time, your faith is likely to be shaken; you will begin to mistrust.

Time

Relationships grow closer and deeper in proportion to the time we allocate to them. Closeness doesn't happen if our time together occurs only when we get everything else done. Intimacy must be one of the things to be done!

If downshifting has given you more free time, building closer relationships is one of the best ways to spend it.

One way to facilitate having more time together is to engage in more shared activities. With your children this might mean more active participation in their school events, with your parents more social visits or short trips together, with friends a shared season ticket to sports arena or theater, and with a spouse or significant other it means dropping some activities that keep you apart and substituting activities that can be done jointly. For instance, if your partner likes to play bridge, learn to play; if you enjoy playing golf, offer your partner professional lessons.

Not only do shared activities allow more time together but they also create bonds and stimulate conversation. Here is an example from my own life:

> One night I received a phone call from the president of our parish council. He asked me to serve on the council as chairman of the family life committee. I said "OK, but only if Dee and I can serve together. We only want one vote, but we want to do it as a couple." There was a moment of stunned silence, and then he said he'd get back to me. An hour later, I imagine after much discussion, the council agreed to our taking the responsibility as a team.

Engaging in this shared activity was stimulating. We would talk for hours about family life ideas that we wanted to put before the council. After the meetings were over, we commiserated together over whatever was rejected and shared in the joyful excitement of our victories. We had a lot to talk about, and we felt close and bonded.

Altered Sense of Privacy

Altering your sense of privacy means being more open with those with whom you want to be more intimate. It involves sharing more deeply what we think and feel and encouraging our loved ones to do likewise. This open sharing creates a haven in our stressful world that keeps the relationship strong despite upsets and crises. Dr. Hugh Leavell, a family therapist writing in the *Palm Beach Post*, succinctly describes this kind of intimacy and how to achieve it:

> To be intimate is to disclose what is internal, to share with another person that which is normally kept within. We cannot be intimate with everyone, nor would we wish to be. Our innermost thoughts and feelings are private and belong only to ourselves. But if we can share them with another person, we can feel connected in a way that alleviates our loneliness.
>
> Most people want this sort of intimacy with their spouse. But they often don't know how to cultivate an intimacy that is comfortable for both parties. Here are a few hints:
>
> - Intimate sharing involves two behaviors—talking and listening. You cannot do both at the same time. But you must be able to do both. Intimacy is a two-way communication.
>
> - The time to listen is when your partner wants to speak. Learn to recognize when this is, and train yourself to be ready. Timing is everything in intimacy.
>
> - Many people have a hard time identifying their own and others' feelings. But this is very important to intimate communication. Develop a vocabulary of feeling words you can use to describe yourself or understand your partner.

- Accept your partner's revelations at face value. Let them know you accept them and respect their position, even if you don't always agree with it. This will help them trust you. Then they'll tell you more. And that's good.

- Avoid offensive and defensive postures. Either one is likely to turn your intimate exchange into a contest.

- Take a few chances. Sure, it's risky to reveal yourself. You might be criticized or even rejected sometimes. That won't kill you. And it could revive a dead or wounded relationship.[5]

Support

I'd like to describe for you now an example of how intimate sharing brought my wife and me closer together. First, you need to know something about me. I am the kind of person who thrives on being able to succeed at whatever I attempt—whether starting a fire in our fireplace or building a successful business. I hate to fail. Failure does a number on me. This is when I really need support.

Last spring we were expecting friends for a weekend cruise on our sailboat. It was late Friday afternoon and most of the work for converting the boat from winter storage to cruising capability was completed, except for the installation of three marine batteries.

Each year, I use a wiring diagram to guide the battery reconnections. This particular afternoon I could not find the diagram. I thought to myself, I've done this for the past four summers, how complicated can it be? I felt impatient to get the boat preparation finished, so I proceeded without the diagram.

Once the hook-up was completed, I turned on the battery switch and *whoosh*, a column of white smoke rose from the alternator! I had wired the batteries incorrectly and blown out the circuits. This meant the weekend cruise was off, I'd have to buy a new alternator, and I was faced with the messy, knuckle-scraping task of removing the old one. I felt devastated at my failure. After awhile, I closed up the boat and went home.

As I walked in the door, my wife said "What's the matter?" I thought that I looked the same as usual and replied "Nothing's the matter." She then said to me, "Well, *something* must be wrong." (How can they tell?) At that moment, I had a decision to make:

1. I could preserve the image of a successful person by explaining to Dee that the alternator burned out and we wouldn't be able to take our friends sailing.

2. I could reveal my inner self—the part of me I hide from most people. I could share with her the negative judgments I was making about myself and the angry and ashamed feelings I was experiencing. I could be open about my failure.

I decided to be candid with Dee and reveal my feelings. I told her, "I'm so upset. I did a stupid thing down at the boat because of my damned impatience—I didn't take enough time to find my wiring diagram. I didn't connect the batteries right and burned out the alternator. The cruise is off. I feel so embarrassed I'd like to disappear. I feel like kicking myself."

Dee listened and then opened her arms and gave me a warm hug. She said "It's OK, Honey, I love you."

That was a special moment. We felt so close. We were filled with tender love for each other; we felt warm and relaxed. We were a couple in love. And it wasn't just for that moment. We were a different couple now; closer than before—more bonded, more in love, and more excited about our relationship.

Imagine how that afternoon might have gone had I chosen not to reveal the judgments and feelings I had inside. Undoubtedly I would have been grouchy and irritable. We probably would have been distant and cool with each other; probably we would both have had a miserable day. Instead, it was wonderful and romantic. After forty years of marriage, we were acting like newlyweds.

The easiest way to experience the joy of knowing you're loved for who you are—for your negative parts as well as the positive—is to open up and let your closest loved ones encounter all of you.

While Dr. Leavell and I focused on intimacy in marriage,

I would encourage you to use newfound time to expand the number of people with whom you have an intimate relationship—including brothers, sisters, friends, and parents. As such relationships strengthen, personal happiness also increases.

WHERE WE'VE BEEN / WHERE WE'RE GOING

This chapter provides a roadmap to insure that your downshifting pays off. We shared psychological research findings about several common characteristics of happy people, with the expectation that we can learn and profit from their experiences.

The most-reported finding was that happy persons have at least one close relationship. We pointed out that building closer relationships helps us feel good about ourselves by (1) fulfilling our need to love and be loved, (2) enhancing our self-esteem, and (3) bringing renewed excitement and romance to existing love relationships.

The chapter introduced the concept of psychological intimacy. Intimate relationships are described as those in which both parties openly reveal to each other their inner selves. When this occurs, a greater bonding and new sense of closeness are experienced. Happiness almost always follows.

Our next chapter brings our journey together to a close. We'll discuss the importance of "seizing the moment," along with practical suggestions for implementing lifestyle changes.

Questions for Reflection

1. What actions could I take that are likely to increase my happiness?

2. How will those I am closest to feel about my ideas for using the newfound time?

3. As I think about the persons with whom I have the closest relationships, to what extent do I typically reveal my inner self (come from behind my mask and share my feelings—my self

doubts, fears, and hurts). What makes it difficult for me to disclose more?

4. As I recall the feelings I experienced when I first fell in love, what was happening in the relationship that produced those feelings?

5. How adequate is the time I now allocate for nurturing and building closer relationships?

6. What are my thoughts and feelings about tapping more extensively into spiritual resources?

CHAPTER 10

YOUR HAPPINESS IS UP TO YOU

I made a living, but I never really lived.

(THE SINGLE MOST COMMON REGRET OF THE TERMINALLY ILL, ACCORDING TO ELISABETH KUBLER-ROSS[1])

THERE'S MORE TO LIFE THAN WORK

Even though we have now come to the end of our journey to-gether, a new, potentially exciting, one is beginning for you. In the preceding chapters we have shown you how to be less controlled by work so that you can find more time for yourself and your loved ones. I hope you have gained the necessary confidence to take fur-ther steps toward working less and enjoying life more. From here on, it's up to you.

If you are saying to yourself, "One of these days I'm going to do something about the way my job controls my life," realize that such thinking leads nowhere. It is important to take some action step *now*, even if it's simply to establish a timetable or to talk with a loved one about your plans. Only you can determine which actions are appropriate. Only you can make the changes that will give you more time to "smell the roses."

If you are at all hesitant about working less, it might be helpful to recall that nobody ever said, while dying, "I wish I had spent more time at work." We've heard that so often, it may no longer have its original power. Take a moment to reflect on it now. For most of us, the comment touches sensitive nerves. We sense the statement's validity; perhaps we experience some uneasiness. We wonder if, on our own deathbed, we might regret the way we allocated our time.

So often it takes a traumatic event to get us to take stock and think about what is really important for our happiness. The event may be a hospital stay, or a spouse that threatens to call it quits, or a child in trouble with the law, or a job loss. Here's just such an example from a John Case column in *The Boston Globe*:

> ". . . one of the great attractions of entrepreneurship. . . [is that] you can spend as much time as you want with your family. Or so runs the myth.
>
> The reality can be agonizingly different.
>
> An entrepreneur named Tom Reisinger finally realized this sad truth when his only child, John, was nearly killed in an auto accident. A 40-ton 18-wheeler nearly flattened the Honda that the 17-year-old boy had been riding in. . . .
>
> Reisinger had managed to ignore—or deny—John's troubles. The falling grades. The marijuana smoking. The fact that John, once a top soccer prospect, had given up sports.
>
> Now John was lying in a hospital bed, suffering from massive internal injuries. And Reisinger could no long avoid the grim conclusion: His business was killing his family. . . .
>
> Reisinger's wife, Margo, tried repeatedly—and failed repeatedly—to get Tom focused on their son's difficulties. Over-stressed, she suffered a nervous breakdown, and was five weeks in the hospital recuperating. John went to boarding school, but was kicked out for drinking and smoking marijuana.
>
> Then—last June—came the wreck. What worsened the tragedy was the fact that it happened two hours away from where John told his parents he would be. . . .

Reisinger has been changing for a while now. The family began seeing a therapist when Margo got back from the hospital. The accident only stiffened his resolve to put them first, rather than business.

Today, Margo is better. John recovered from his injuries, attended an Outward Bound-type program, finished his junior year in home schooling, and won his way back to the boarding school that expelled him. . . .

Reisinger may not yet be the ideal father. But he has learned a lot. Courageously, he has also told his story to a national magazine in hopes that it will help other entrepreneurs avoid the all-too-common trap of sacrificing a family on the altar of a business.[2]

Fortunately, it needn't take situations like this to help us look at what we are doing with our lives. The fact that you've read this book puts you clearly ahead of the pack. I hope that the steps you initiate now will enable you to enjoy more fully all that life has to offer, both for your self and those you care about.

Here's a way to begin. Examine the checklist, "Steps I Can Take to Begin Downshifting." It provides a variety of action steps. Check all those you believe should have priority. The list is segmented for easier review, but mix-and-match, or combinations of items, might be ideal for you. For example, you might choose designing a job-sharing arrangement that also includes telecommuting.

STEPS I CAN TAKE TO BEGIN DOWNSHIFTING

Making the Decision

_____ Set aside quiet time for reflection about my current lifestyle and what to do about it.

_____ Talk with loved ones about cutting back.

_____ Quietly explore how others in the company have reduced their workload.

_____ Get more information on my organization's policies re: flextime, part-time work, reduced hours, longer vacations, etc.

_____ Decide on how much risk I am willing to take—from little or none to "If I get fired, so be it."

_____ Decide on timing. When will I publicly announce my desires?

_____ Determine if my changes can be separated into steps or stages so I can make an easier transition.

Downshifts to Consider—Changing My Work Patterns

Clearly, some of the following possibilities may not be appropriate in your circumstances. Moreover, at the outset it may be prudent to proceed slowly. Which of the following, if any, might represent a worthwhile change?

_____ Keep my lunchtime personal.

_____ Set more reasonable deadlines.

_____ Say no to some projects.

_____ Overtly declare my family as #1 priority.

_____ Reduce weekend business travel.

_____ Make personal appointments as firm as work ones.

_____ Take family with me on business trip.

_____ Set a "stop line" (a specific hour to leave work).

_____ Ask for extra vacation time.

_____ Move closer to work.

Downshifts to Consider—Changing Work Arrangements

_____ Alter your hours of work—a flextime arrangement.

_____ Work part-time.

_____ Telecommute one day or more per week.

_____ Work out a job-sharing arrangement.

_____ Retire early.

_____ Retire gradually.

_____ Seek a lateral move to a less demanding job.

_____ Decline a promotion (if it requires greater time commitment).

_____ Downshift to a less demanding job.

Making Best Use of New Found Time

_____ Involve self in more family activities.

_____ Make time for deeper, more open communication with loved ones.

_____ Establish new relationships.

_____ Heal a relationship (asking/giving forgiveness).

_____ Devote more time to my health—for example, regular exercise regimen.

_____ Devote more time/effort to reaching out to others.

_____ Devote more time for education and self-development.

_____ Nurture/renew neglected relationships.

_____ Volunteer to help some group of interest to you.

_____ Make better use of spiritual resources.

WHAT IF I'M AMBIVALENT?

You might _want_ to make a change, but you're feeling uncomfortable about it. That's normal. All of us experience anxiety when we are about to make a significant decision. For most of us, it appears that there are risks involved in giving less time to career and more to self or family.

By nature, many of us are hard driving. This is the way we approach life, especially at work. We wonder if we could behave otherwise. Others of us wonder if we'll have a job if we try to reduce either the hours or the effort given to it. Workaholics will have an especially difficult time trying to shape a better balance between work and the rest of their life.

There is no simple answer I can give. It comes down to the question of what "life success" means to you. The best indicator that at least *some* change is appropriate is the extent to which you presently feel discontented or uneasy. If you desire more contentment, the risks in making a change are probably worth it.

One reassuring piece of research was recently reported in *The New York Times*. Judith Dobrzynski[3] described a study by Peter Capelli, a management professor at the Wharton School. He and his co-researchers found that men who had placed high importance on both finding the right spouse and having a good family life earned, on the average, more than those who did not. For women, the same correlations existed, but they were weaker.

The researchers further found little or no relationship between earnings and the importance placed on money or success at work.

Ms. Dobrzynski's article states that Capelli "would like to see a rethinking of the assumed tradeoff between work and family. He believes that people should think about time invested in good family life the way they now think of time spent on exercise: it takes time that might be spent at work, but it also pays dividends for the employee and employer."

As Professor Capelli put it: "The alternative to a good family life is not no family life; it's bad family life." Ann Landers provides an example of the professor's thinking:

DEAR ANN LANDERS: This is in response to "Burnt Out," who worked killer hours, never saw his family, and was hanging on by his fingernails. I was in the same boat, putting in 60 hours a week, taking work home, bypassing days off and neglecting my family—all for $65,000 a year. I had worked in the same Fortune 500 company for over 18 years. It was the only job I'd ever had, and I was afraid to quit. I had received many awards and bonuses, but I was exhausted, overweight, depressed, and spending over $12,000 a year on therapy.

One day, I heard a phrase that changed my life: "Fear will not harm you, but the fear of failure will." That made me think seriously about quitting my job. Finally, I did.

I am now making less than half of what I used to make, but I feel like a different person. I put in 40 hours a week and never take work home; my weekends are mine to do with as I please, and I am becoming reacquainted with my wife and family. I am no longer in therapy because the depression has left me.

It was a big adjustment, and there are times I miss the big bucks, but I know this was the right decision for me. Ann, tell your readers that "stop and smell the roses" may be just a cliché, but I know what those roses smell like, and it's heaven. —Somewhere in Ohio

DEAR OHIO: What you did took a tremendous amount of courage. I'll bet your wife was behind you 100% and she doesn't mind living on a lot less. She now has a husband who is healthier and happier, and the kids have a dad. Too often big money isn't worth what you have to do to get it. —Ann Landers[4] *(Used by permission of Creators Syndicate)*

YOUR FUTURE

No one knows what the future holds in store for you. Not you, not your spouse, not your friends. The only thing we know for certain is that there will be change. You will change; the world around you will change.

Five years from today, many things that now seem important to you are very likely to be perceived as unimportant. Five years from now, you may not even be here!

We don't have forever to balance our lives or find the contentment we desire. The best maybe yet to come, but *now* is the time we need to begin.

Making changes in your work life will not be easy. If it were easy, you probably would have made some of them long ago. It takes courage, conviction, and trust in your judgment. To help make your lifestyle change efforts productive, here are a few time-proven guidelines:

1. *Attempt one change at a time.* This helps you focus your efforts. For example, if you have gained approval to make a lateral move and also want to telecommute, don't simultaneously attempt both. Instead, get settled and become successful in the new job before implementing plans for telecommuting.

2. *Start with changes that are relatively simple.* Examine the possibilities for breaking your planned change into easily managed phases or steps and take it one step at a time. For example, suppose you've set a goal to carve out more personal time during the workweek. You might begin by setting aside a particular day of the week, say Wednesday, for keeping your lunch hour free for personal use. Once you have that pattern established to your satisfaction, extend the concept to two days, eventually working up to a goal of four such lunch hours per week.

   If you've decided to begin building closer, more intimate relationships with those closest to you, success is more likely if you begin by focusing your efforts on one person rather than two or more.

3. *Involve someone else.* It's helpful to have someone to report to—someone who knows and cares—to remind us, be our conscience, to provide encouragement, and to give us an occasional kick in the pants. Consider involving your spouse, friend, secretary, co-worker, or boss—depending upon the nature of the change.

4. *Put time-boundaries on the change effort.* For example, it is ineffective to say "From now on I'm going to set more reasonable deadlines for myself." Most people find it difficult to focus energy on a "from now on I'll do. . ." basis. It's more productive to say "During next week, I am going to look at each demand that is asked of me and make sure the deadline I accept is reasonable."

If your change begins producing the desired results, make a pact with yourself to continue the effort for another week. If things did not work as you expected, review how you attempted to implement the change, revise if necessary, and try once more. Or, you may discover that the selected change is not for you and that another alternative might be more beneficial.

The important thing is, *don't give up.* Success in changing almost always involves trial-and-error learning. Recognize, at the outset, that changing is a process—one of trying, adjusting, trying, adjusting. The rewards will be worth the effort.

PARTING COMPANY

As I leave you, my fondest wish is that you have the resolve to take the road less traveled, to act on your convictions, to take the risk, to be more the authentic you, and in these ways find the happiness you desire for yourself and your loved ones. Your quest for success defined by simplicity, love, and meaningfulness, in a world that defines success as material gain, is truly a hero's journey. But those who have tasted the fruits of such a journey find the rewards more than worth the effort. Go for it!

If you have any suggestions for future editions of this book, or wish to share with me the story of your downshifting efforts, I would be most pleased to hear from you.

John D. Drake
P.O. Box 1516
Kennebunkport, ME 04046
e-mail: drake5546@cybertours.com

Group Discussions

This book lends itself to workshops or group discussions about achieving a more balanced life. For your convenience, the Appendix provides a brief study guide to facilitate group discussions. I hope that you and your friends find it helpful in bringing more pleasure, peace, and passion into your life.

Questions for Self Reflection

1. What am I waiting for?

2. Suppose I do nothing about cutting back, what are the consequences?

3. What is my dream for my family and myself? (Consider sharing it with those you love.)

GROUP DISCUSSION GUIDE
A FIVE-SESSION PROGRAM

OVERVIEW

Purpose:

To aid participants in finding a better balance in their lives by helping them make the transition to a less work-focused lifestyle.

Format

This is a suggested format for five 2-hour group discussions. When ten or more participants are involved, it is recommended that participants break into groups of approximately six persons. Group discussions can then be more productive. The number of sessions and their duration can easily be modified to accommodate the participants' schedules and needs.

Basically, the format of each meeting consists of the following steps:

1.   *Reading* designated sections of the book (participants take turns reading aloud and others follow along in their books).

2.   *Group discussion.* Questions are provided and all are encouraged to share in responding (about 20 minutes).

3.   *Personal reflection.* Participants write privately about the way the issues being discussed are relevant to their own lives (about 10 minutes).

4.   *Group sharing.* On a voluntary basis, participants share a portion of their written thoughts and reactions (about 20 minutes)

5.   *Set date.* Plan time and location of next session.

For most sessions, the procedures described above are typically repeated twice during a session. Each part focuses on a different aspect of downshifting.

SESSION ONE

Downshifting—Is It for Me?

A.   *Introductions.* Unless participants are well acquainted, each person introduces self by providing:

1.   Name

2.   Family situation (single, married, children, etc.)

3.   Where employed and current position

4.   What is hoped to gain from the discussions

B.   *Readings.* Read aloud all of the first paragraph on page 19.

C.   *Group discussion* (allow about 20 minutes for each question).

"What are your biggest concerns about cutting back time spent at work?"

"Considering both yourself and those you love, what do you see as the most important benefits from downshifting?"

D.   *Private writing and reflection.* "What are my most significant fears about downshifting? How can I get past them?"

E.   *Voluntary Sharing.* Participants share their written reflections.

F.   *Set date.* Plan for next session.

SESSION TWO

Making the Decision—Moving Ahead

Part 1

    A. *Readings.* Chapter 4, pages 38–41 (up to "If You're Still on the Fence."

    B. *Group discussion.* "What ways have you found helpful to make an important decision?"

    C. *Personal writing and reflection.* "How helpful would it be to set up a family meeting to discuss my downshifting? Who would I involve? When? Where?"

    D. *Voluntary sharing* on reflections.

Part 2

    A. *Readings.* Page 48, first paragraph under the heading "Changing the Way You Work." Page 55, read checklist of options.

    B. *Group discussion.* "Which, if any, of the ten suggestions appeal to you? Why?"

    C. *Personal writing and reflection.* "When I think about making some change in the way I work, what troubles me the most? What could I do to reduce the concern?"

    D. *Voluntary sharing* of personal reflections.

    E. *Set date for next session.*

SESSION 3

Moving Ahead: Bigger Gains & Selling My Plan

Part 1

    A. *Readings.* Page 57–58 up to "Arrange for Flextime" heading.

    B. *Group discussion.* "Of the eight options presented, which ones, if any, struck a responsive note and led you to think, 'I might like to try that.'"

    C. *Personal writing and reflection.* "When would be the best time to begin efforts at downshifting (whether low risk or high risk)? What are my risks in delaying?"

    D. *Voluntary sharing* of personal reflections.

Part 2

A. *Readings.* Page 71, first paragraph; Pages 73–74, Section entitled, "Put It in Writing."

B. *Group discussion.* "What do you intend to do, within your company, to maximize the likelihood that your request to downshift will be accepted?"

C. *Personal writing and reflection.* "What or who in my organization is likely to present problems in granting my downshifting request? What can I do about it? Who in my family will need to be convinced? What can I do about it?"

D. *Voluntary sharing* of personal reflections.

E. *Set date for next session.*

SESSION 4

The Rewards—Enjoying Life More

Part 1

A. *Readings.* Pages 89–91 up to section headed "1. Happy people engage in activities they enjoy."

B. *Group discussion.* "If, after downshifting, you have new-found time, what actions could you take to increase your happiness?"

C. *Personal writing and reflection.* "How will those I am closest to feel about my ideas for using the new-found time?"

D. *Voluntary sharing* of personal reflections.

Part 2

A. *Readings.* Starting on page 95 at the heading entitled, "5. Happy people nurture at least one close, intimate relationship" to "Obstacles to Intimacy" on page 96.

B. *Group discussion.* "What do you think it takes to build closer, more intimate relationships with those you care most about?"

C. *Personal writing and reflection.* "How adequate is the time I now allocate for nurturing and building closer relationships with those I care most about? What am I willing to do to improve the situation?"

D. *Voluntary sharing* of personal reflections.

E. *Set date for next session.*

SESSION 5

It's Up to You

A. *Readings.* Pages 107–109 to the end of the story of Tom Reisinger.

B. *Group discussion.* "Right now, where are you at with taking some action now to downshift?"

C. *Personal Writing and Reflection.* Complete the checklist on pages 109 to 111. "Of the items I checked, which ones do I want to initiate within the next 2 months?"

D. *Voluntary Sharing.* Share on personal reflections.

E. *Wrap Up Group Discussion.* "How can we help each other to implement our downshifting?"

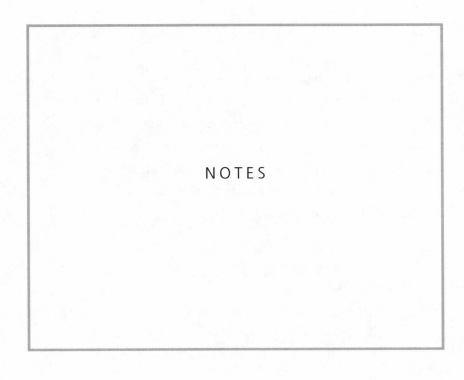

NOTES

Chapter 1: Is This Any Way to Live?

1. Amy Saltzman. "When Less is More," *U.S. News and World Report*, October 27, 1997.

2. Gates McKibben. Based on personal correspondence with the author, 2000.

3. Lauren R. Rublin. "Too, Too Much," *Barrons*, March 9, 1998.

4. Bradley Foss. "Simplicity Itself," *Maine Sunday Telegram*, December 5, 1999.

Chapter 2: The Work Trap

1. Barrie Greiff and Preston Hunter. Tradeoffs: *Executive, Family, and Organizational Life*, New York: New American Library, 1980.

2. Janet Wittenauer. Direct quote from personal interview with author, 2000.

Chapter 3: What's Stopping You?

1. Laurence J. Peters. *Peter's Quotations*, New York, Morrow, 1993.

2. Sebastian Yates. Personal interview with the author, 1999.

3. Regina Trombitas. Personal correspondence with the author, 1999.

4. Delia Regan. Personal interview with the author, 2000.

5. George Ostler. Personal interview with the author, 1998.

6. Gail Sheehy. *Passages*, New York, Bantam, 1984.

Chapter 5: Low-Risk Downshifting Options

1. Amy Saltzman. "When Less Is More," *U.S. News and World Report*, October 27, 1997.

2. Elaine St. John. *Simplify Your Life*, New York, Hyperion, 1994.

3. Bob Duncan. Based on personal interview with the author, 1999.

Chapter 6: Riskier Steps Toward the Life You Want

1. Bob Baum. "Family Comes First," *Portland Press Herald*, December 14, 1999.

2. John Carlisle. Based on personal correspondence with the author, 2000.

3. Maggie Jackson. "Telecommuting Grows Rapidly," *Portland Press Herald*, July 4, 1997.

4. Arlene Hirsch. *Love Your Work and Success Will Follow*, New York, Wiley, 1989.

5. Dave Ketcher. Personal interview with the author, 1999.

6. Donns K. H. Walters. "Portfolio Careers Replacing 'the Job'," *Maine Sunday Telegram*, June 4, 1995.

Chapter 7: Getting Your Organization's Buy-In

1. Noel Tichy and Stratford Sherman. *Control Your Destiny or Someone Else Will*, New York, Harper Business, 1999.

2. Edward Dolnick. "Trade Money for Time," *Health*, October, 1994.

Chapter 8: When the Answer Is No

1. Laurence J. Peters. *Peter's Quotations*, New York, Morrow, 1993.

2. Susan Arledge. Based on personal correspondence with the author, 2000.

3. Richard Leider and David Shapiro. *Repacking Your Bags*, San Francisco, Berrett-Koehler, 1996.

Chapter 9: You Did It!

1. Laurence J. Peters. *Peter's Quotations*, New York, Morrow, 1993.

2. Tom Himple. Based on personal interview with the author, 1998.

3. American Heart Association, advertisement, *Maine Sunday Telegram*, September 5, 1999.

4. St. Augustine. *Restless 'Till We Rest in You*, Ann Arbor, MI, Servant Publications, 1998.

5. Hugh Leavell. "Follow These Tips for a Healthy Family," *Palm Beach Post*, March 25, 1994.

Chapter 10: Your Happiness Is Up to You

1. Elisabeth Kübler-Ross, *On Death and Dying*, New York, Collier, 1997.

2. John Case. "Successful Entrepreneur, Lousy Parent?" *Boston Globe*, February 8, 1995.

3. Judith Dobrzynski. "Should I Have Left for Home an Hour Earlier?" *The New York Times*, June 18, 1995.

4. Ann Landers. "He Got Off the Treadmill and Smelled the Roses," *Portland Press Herald*, January 4, 1995.

SUGGESTED READINGS

Your Career

Cabrera, James C. and Charles F. Albrecht. *The Lifetime Career Manager*. Holbrook, MA: Adams Media, 1995.

Drake, John D. *The Perfect Interview—How to Get the Job You Really Want*. New York: Amacon, 1997.

Lucht, John. *Rites of Passage at $100,000 +*. New York: Viceroy, 1991.

Lucht, John. *Executive Job Changing Workbook*. New York: Viceroy, 1994.

Nemko, Marty and Paul and Sarah Edwards. *Cool Careers for Dummies*. New York: IDG/MacMillan, 1998.

Sinetar, Marsha. *Do What You Love, the Money Will Follow*. New York: Dell, 1987.

Your Happiness

Carlson, Richard. *Don't Sweat the Small Stuff.... and It's All Small Stuff*. New York: Hyperion, 1997.

Powell, John. *Happiness Is an Inside Job*. Allen, TX: Tabor, 1989.

St. James, Elaine. *Simplify Your Life*. New York: Hyperion, 1994.

Setting Priorities

Dominquey, Joe and Vicki Robbins. *Your Money or Your Life: Transforming Your Relationship with Money and Achieving Financial Independence*. New York: Penguin, 1999.

Helldorfer, Martin C. *Work Trap—Rediscovering Leisure, Redefining Work*. Mystic, CT: Twenty-Third Publications, 1995.

Kübler-Ross, Elisabeth. *On Death and Dying*. New York: Macmillan, 1969.

Leider, Richard J. *Life Skills: Taking Charge of Your Personal and Professional Growth*. San Diego: Pfeiffer, 1994.

Leider, Richard J. and David A. Shapiro. *Repacking Your Bags*. San Francisco: Berrett-Koehler, 1996.

Peck, M. Scott. *The Road Less Traveled*. New York: Simon & Schuster, 1978.

Spirituality

Powell, John. *Through Seasons of the Heart*. Allen, TX: Tabor, 1987.

Thompson, Francis. *The Hound of Heaven*. New York: McCracken, 1993.

Job Sharing

Meirer, Gretl S. *A New Pattern for Quality of Work and Life W. E*. Kalamazoo, MI: Upjohn, 1979.

Early Retirement

Abromovitz, Les. *You Can Retire While You're Still Young Enough to Enjoy It*. Chicago: Dearborn Trade, 1999.

Gilbert, Edward. *How to Retire Early and Live Well with Less Than a Million Dollars*. Holbrook, MA: Adams Media, 2000.

Wasik, John F. *Retire Early and Live the Life You Want Now: A 10-Step Plan for Reinventing Retirement*. New York: Holt, 2000.

Meditation/Retreats

Bodian, Stephan. *Meditation for Dummies*. New York: IDG/MacMillan, 1999.

Davich, Victor N. and Jack Canfield. *The Best Guide to Meditation*. Los Angeles: Audio Renaissance, 1998.

Fishel, Ruth. *Precious Solitude*. Holbrook, MA: Adams Media, 1999.

Jones, Timothy K. *A Place for God: A Guide for Spiritual Retreats and Retreat Centers*. New York: Doubleday, 2000.

Kelly, Jack and Marcia. *Sanctuaries the Complete United States: A Guide to Lodging in Monasteries, Abbeys, and Retreats*. New York: Bell Tower, 1996.

Roche, Lorin. *Meditation Made Easy*. New York: Harper San Francisco, 1998.

Telecommuting

Anderson, Sandy. *The Work at Home Balancing Act: The Professional Resource Guide for Managing Yourself, Your Work, and Your Family at Home*. New York: Avon, 1998.

Dimocenzo, Debra A. and Ronald C. Fetzer. *101 Tips for Telecommuting: Successfully Manage Your Work, Team, Technology, and Family*. San Francisco: Berrett-Koehler, 1999.

Shaw, Lisa. *Telecommute: Go to Work Without Leaving Home*. New York: Wiley, 1996.

INDEX

130

ABOUT THE AUTHOR

John D. Drake currently serves as chairman of the board of Drake Inglesi Milardo, Inc. Before creating this firm, Drake founded and served as CEO of Drake Beam & Associates, Inc. (now Drake Beam Morin, Inc.), the world's largest human resources consulting firm (200+ offices in 43 countries). John Drake chose to downshift and sold his firm to a major publishing company.

Over the past thirty years, Drake served as consultant to America's Fortune 500 companies, including AT&T, Atlantic Richfield, Citibank, GTE, Prudential Insurance, Warner-Lambert, and the World Bank. He is well known in corporate circles as a psychologist, consultant, speaker, and author.

Drake has served as trustee for the University of New England. He holds a Ph.D. in counseling psychology from Case-Western Reserve University, an MA in psychology from Fordham University, and a BS in economics and psychology from Rutgers University. Drake has been awarded diplomate status by the American Board of Examiners in Professional Psychology.

Earlier in his career, Dr. Drake was the director of psychological services for Dunlap and Associates and director of management development for Allied-Signal Corporation.

John and Dee Drake were married in 1952 and have four sons. They divide their time between Maine and Florida.